SQUATCHLAND II

Under the Sign of the Crooked Snake

AUTHOR:

DAVID HOLLIS

(Unknown Primate Studies | 2018-2022)

Leavitt Peak Press

ISBN: 978-1-961017-41-2 (sc)
ISBN: 978-1-961017-42-9 (e)

Rev. date: 06/06/2023

Contents

Preface 1

Chapter 1 Scar: the leader of the Adecca (Deer)Clan of the Crooked Snake Tribe....................3

Chapter 2 The Mookwarruh (Spirit Talker, or Telepath) Clan 0f Fish Creek and Devil's Brake. 23

Chapter 3 The Nocona Clan (wandering) of Upper Fish Creek and Panther Bayou of the Crooked Snake Tribe 29

Chapter 4 The Tekwapi Clan (no meat eaters) of Clear Creek 39

Chapter 5 Clan of the Lance (Spear) of the Crooked Snake Tribe of Dartigo Creek Valley ...47

Chapter 6 Hunting Tactics, Tools_and Weapons 61

Chapter 7 8- foot Trails and Arches. 68

Chapter 8 Brutus comes to visit. 83

Chapter 9 Ashanti photobombs me...94

Chapter 10 The Cold Irony 99

Chapter 11 Historical Evidence 106

About the Author: 129

I began writing this book within a month of writing my first book, (*The Mystery of the Iatt Lake Monster-Revealed!*) subtitled (*Squatchland- The Dartigo Creek Valley Project*), which told of my moving to Central Louisiana in the fall of 2016 and within months I experienced a violent encounter with a large male Sasquatch after I feared that my dog had been nabbed by them. After making my intentions clear I was able to retrieve my dog and build respect as I was fearless in the face of danger as I experienced a tree push down, a bluff charge through the brush and a stand- off. I told the big male that I was not scared and that we could become good friends if he doesn't hurt my dog.

The next day I worked on finding where they slept during the day so that I could get a picture of them. Within a week I had made my way down to the swamp where they sleep on islands out in the swamp. This swamp is created by three crooked creeks that wind together to form a large clean, and clear swamp, damned by a mile- wide beaver damn with a waterfall forming one creek. When I approached the swamp, I found an 18-inch footprint filling up with water. Then I took what may be the best picture I have taken so far, the picture of a female with a baby on her side.

Then I began making friends with a Sasquatch I named Brutus. I learned that there are differences in the types of what I call Bigfoots in general. Brutus is 8-foot-tall and weighs around 700 pounds. As my friendship with Brutus grew, I noticed Bigfoots paying more attention to me and wanting to be seen and acknowledged also. Now they have followed me to my house on the other side of the parish confirming to me that they all talk to each other and the word has gotten out about me, even though I moved more than 30 miles away! After taking hundreds of pictures daily from my front porch I finally went across the road to see and meet them. That is where my new story begins.

As in my first book, I prefaced my experience level by saying that I hold no relevant degrees on the subject matter and all of my recollections on the subject matter are based on my observations and direct daily contact with hairy biped relic hominids that we suspect are known as Bigfoot, which actually are a variety of different beings that live with, hunt with and hide together as a group. I grew up hunting and fishing with my father in Louisiana and honed my observational and tracking skills in the field. Observation is what this book is based on.

Chapter 1

Scar: the leader of the Adecca (Deer) Clan of the Crooked Snake Tribe

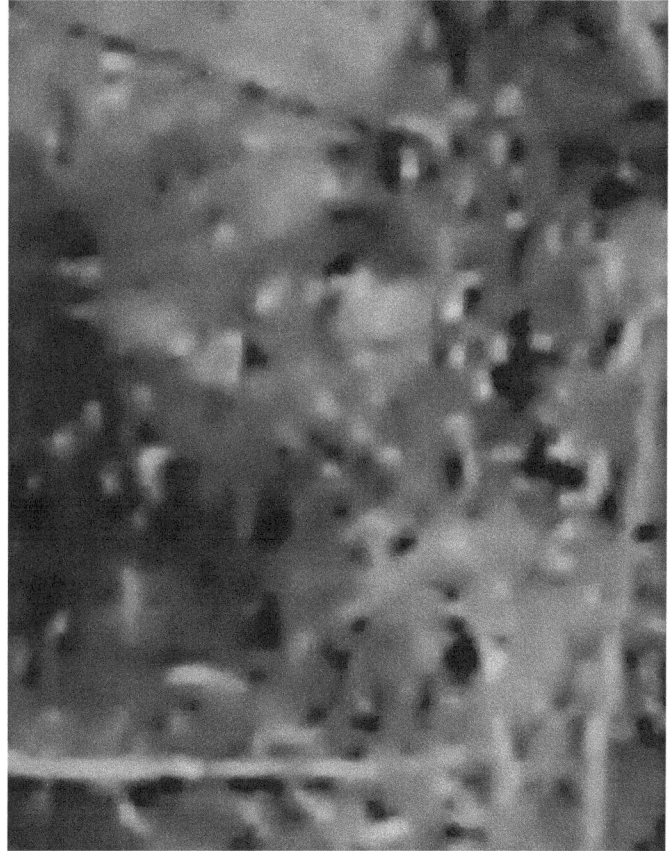

Scar is on the top right of the picture. Below a close- up of Scar.

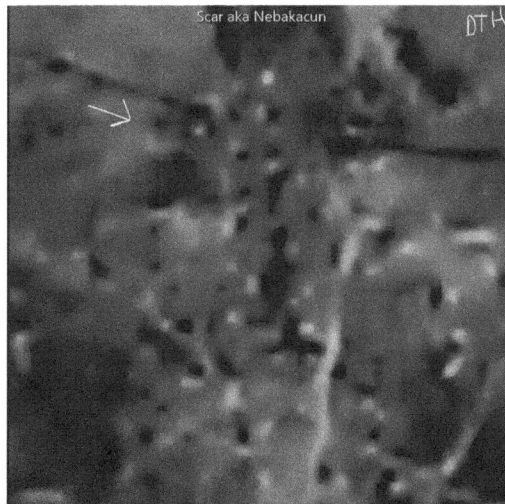

I decided I was going to walk across the road and build a fire. I would then sit by the fire and roll some cigarettes, fire one up, and then say," would you like one"? I did just that, ignoring the bigfoots that were there. I built a medium fire then began rolling cigarettes. I could see in my peripheral sight that they became interested when I pulled out the tobacco and began rolling. I then fired up a cigarette and said the word, Arikara?, which in Comanche means a twist of tobacco. I lifted my hand to hand one out and a very large male Bigfoot stepped up to take the cigarette from my hand. I then looked up and placed my gaze upon him and smiled. He smiled back. I offered him a seat and he sat down on the other side of the fire. I said the word fuego (fire) and offered to light it for him. I took it from him and lit it and handed it back. I told him to take a small hit and showed him how which he did a few times until he coughed. I slapped him on the back until quit coughing and the we laughed for a few minutes. I asked him what his name is and told him my name is David, He said his name is Nabehkakun, which means many fights or many battles. He spoke some English words as well as Comanche, and Chippewa, Sioux and Apache as well as Bigfoot. I asked him where he got the scar on the side of his face and he repeated Nabehkakun and raised his hands as if boxing and I understood. I stood up and went over to Scar and placed my hand on his head and told him that I name you Scar, a powerful name! Scar was taller than me sitting down than I was standing. I am 6 foot 2 inches. He must be between 13 to 14 foot tall. I then pulled out a bag of small candy bars that had a lot of peanuts and pulled open the wrapper on one and sniffed it. Scar started sniffing so I gave him one and encouraged him to take it. I said the word Pena which means sweets in Comanche. He tore it open and smelled it. He put it in his mouth and chewed slowly and then smiled. I pulled out the large bag and started throwing them out and I told him to let the babies come and get some. It was a big hit! I told scar that I wanted to hug a baby and he told a female something in a language something like Chinese, real fast and with some clicking noises also. The Bigfoot woman brought a young cute little girl and Scar handed her to me and said her name is Mo Pe which means owl. I gave her a hug and made a big show out of it. I sat her down in front of me and gave her a blessing and said a prayer over her asking for God's blessing. They all smiled. I told them I would come back many times and soon. I shook Scar's huge hand and lit a few cigarettes before I left and gave them out.

I took this picture before I went inside. A bigfoot is smoking a cigarette to the right of this picture, there is a plume. I would end up going over to the little woods across the road many times. My tobacco and candy expenditures have increased tremendously. Scar told me a lot about his territory, his tribe, and the different clans and their locations. He also told me that I had become a legend after making friends with Brutus the Sasquatch who is feared even among the Bigfoots as the Sasquatches are superior in making weapons and using them. Scar told me that they belong to the Crooked Snake Tribe of which are many clans. Scar's Clan is the Adecca which means Deer Clan in Comanche. Their territory covers Hall Hollow Branch to Mill Creek. Here is a map of the area.

Scar's band has about 500 including the children. Around 100 of them are in my yard as there is a spring in my yard and one next door on my neighbor's yard. Scar said that the women and children stay here mostly while the men go hunting. They trust me and like me and they know it is safe here in my yard. There is fresh water and their hunting grounds are nearby. Those are the reasons so many Bigfoots are in my yard. Here they are lining up to get candy.

 I love it as I get to take pictures from my front porch! They are spoiling me! Even when I leave the house they line up on the roads as they hear my car pulling up. I feel like a tourist driving thru Yellowstone, taking pictures of the wildlife from the car. The following Pictures are from my truck on the road near my home in Scar's territory.

On top of Hall Hill

From Hall Hollow

As I mentioned before in my 1st book, almost all pictures of these creatures are fuzzy. They all pile up on each other, so it is hard to distinguish any one shape, and they use camouflage such as vines, brush and leaves to hide themselves.

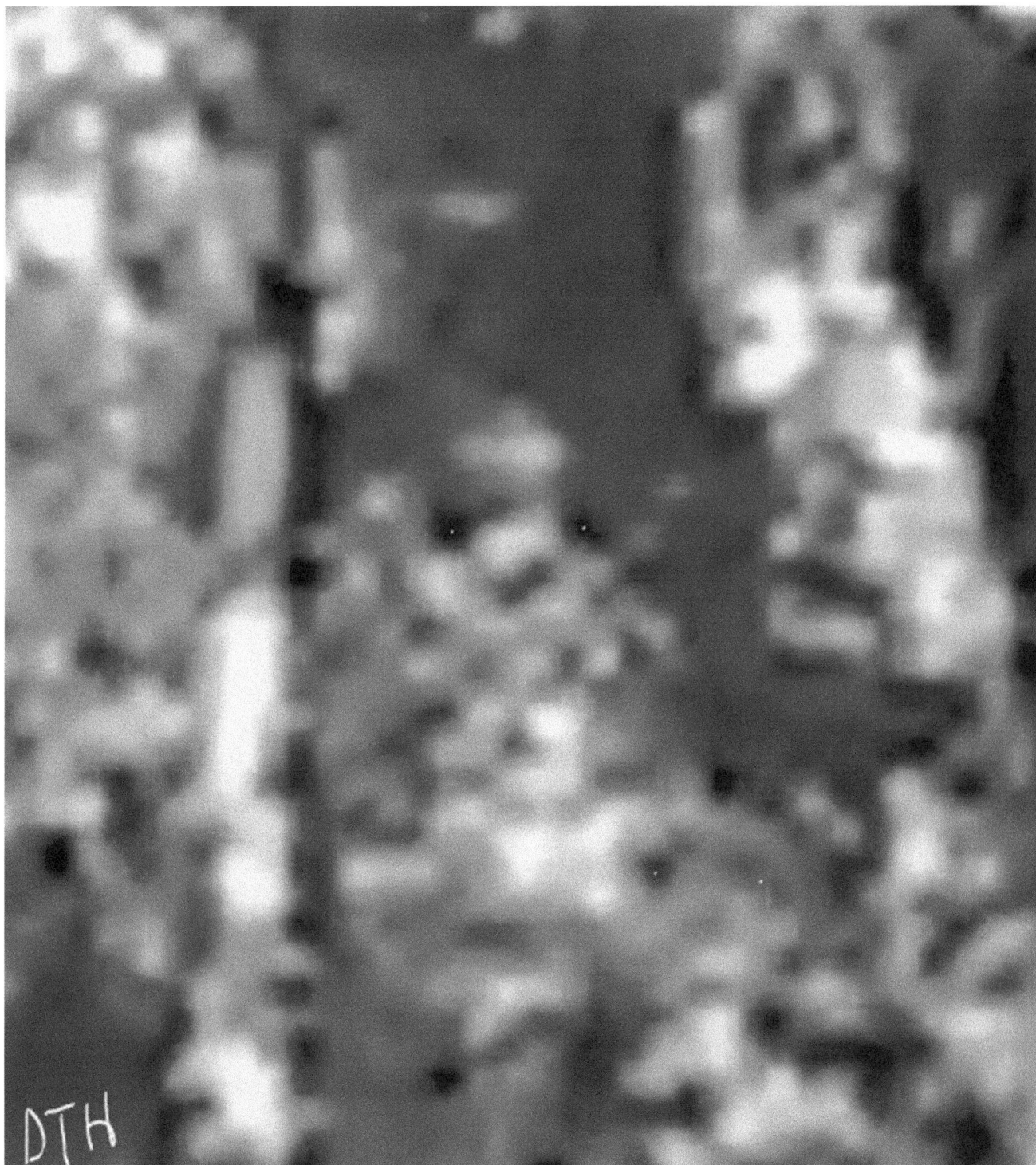

From the road in the car on Hall Hill, Kisatchie National Forest.

Here is a very unusual grouping of unknown Bi-Peds or they could be Bigfoots that have Leprosy. This road is in Kisatchie National Forest and what you are looking at is groundbreaking!

I feel so blessed that God has allowed me to see such things. I must drive down this road when the train is blocking my home, so it is natural for me to be on it. I do not go looking for Bigfoot anymore. They come out to the road for me. Here they have taken over this abandoned house on Hall Hill. Look for the faces.

They like to hide but if you can find the faces in this picture you will notice that all eyes are upon me.

From Hall Hollow

There are many in this picture, in the center of the stream bed.

Well, I made it home after having to drive around thru the woods to get home because of the train. My Friends hear me coming.

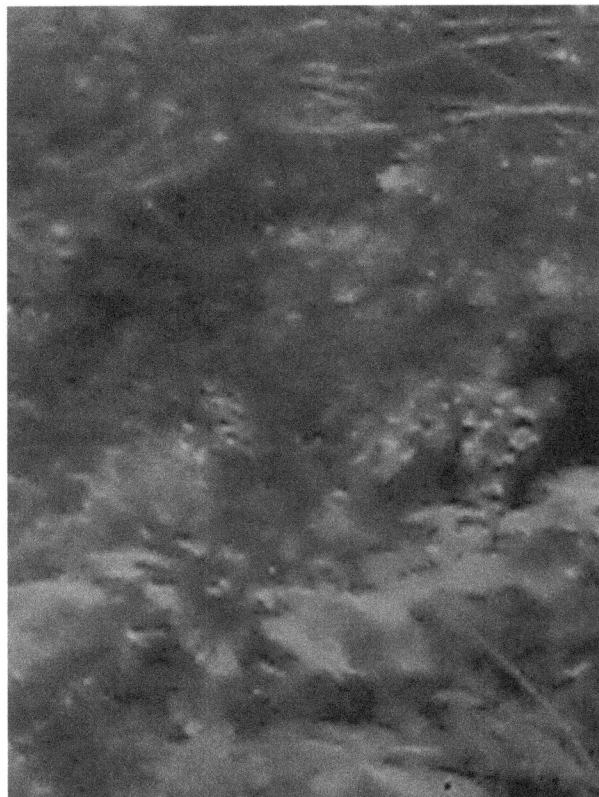

Peeking in my window.

One day I think I am going to install a Bigfoot Cam where folks can go online and view these guys in the moment, live!

Let's move to the other side of the tree. In between the tree and over to the right.

Do you see Blue Man over to the right?

Look for the eyes, then you can find the faces. I live next door to neighbors, so they hide.

Later in the evening they become much more visible as it is less of a chance of them being seen by my neighbors. As identified in my 1st book, these are Skunk Apes.

A very large Giant woman, 13ft tall.

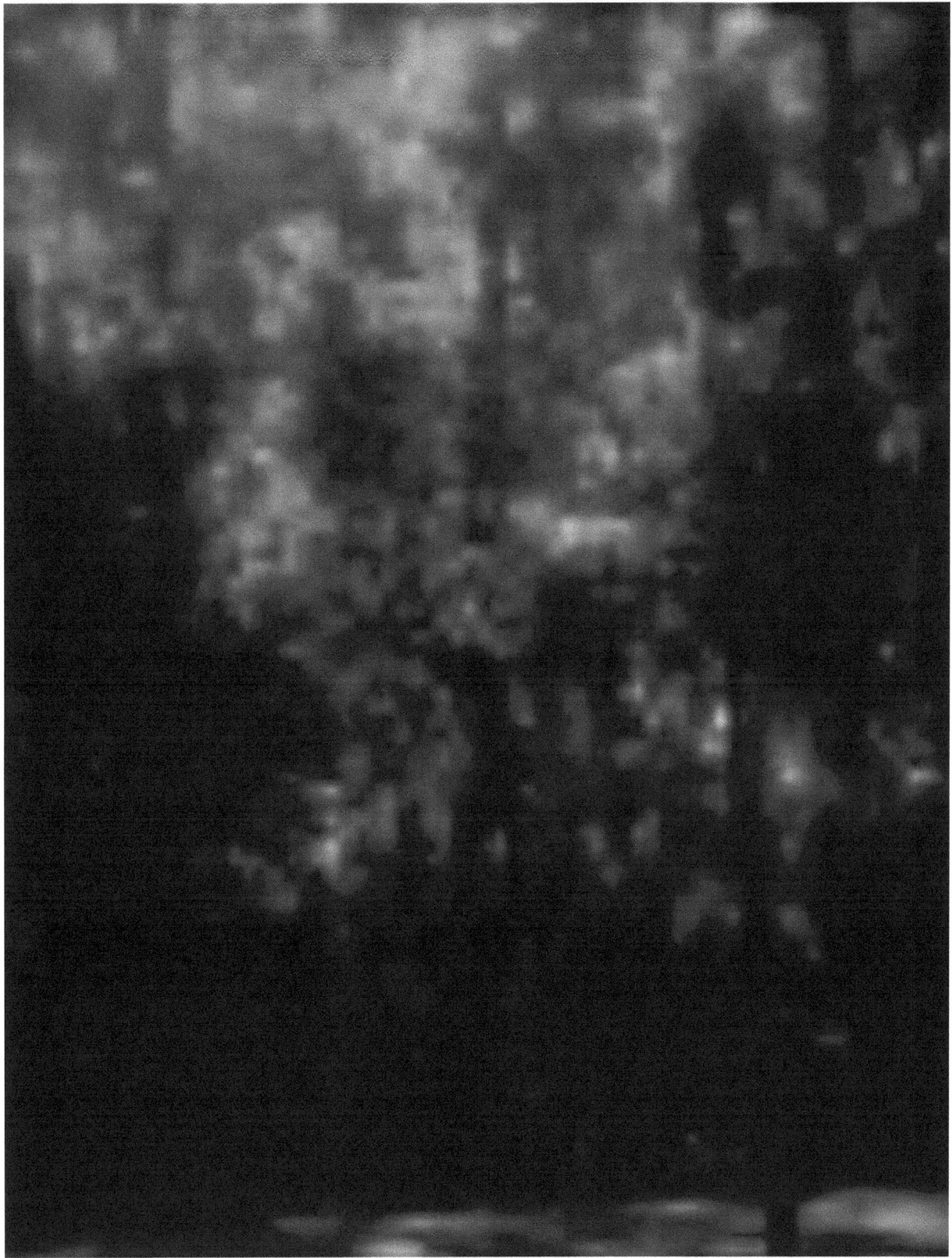

Scar told me that one reason they like me is I knew they were there, and I showed no fear. They fear a fearful man as they are more likely to get shot and because I do not fear them, they feel good about living here on my land, in the little strip of woods, between the railroad tracks, and the road in front of my house.

Although, not all of them stay over across the street. Some of them are so enamored by me they try to see how close they can get to me, desperate for my attention, or they just want to be close to me. This Bigfoot is in my side yard.

Behind the crepe myrtle on this side of the road; a female with large breasts is sitting on a male's shoulders.

Fish Creek is ruled by a council of elders and is a major religious and feast site for the Crooked Snake Tribe and all the local clans of the tribe make their way here a few times a year. I found a tree marked with a crooked snake and the head of the snake had a delta triangle shaped head. I have seen altar stones shaped like this on two islands that are unapproachable to humans. One Island is in the middle of Dartigo Swamp, and the other near the junction of Fish Creek and Little River. Both Islands are heavily guarded and off limits to humans. The elders do not have much of an affinity for me and Scar warned me about going in to far if I go back there. I have a couple of pictures of the sacrificial island near Fish Creek and Devil's Brake.

This picture shows the approach to the sacrificial island at Fish Creek. It is guarded by many Bigfoots and a Shaman. The Altar is to the right which is a large stone shaped like a delta triangle.

The next picture is further to the right showing more of the altar stone. Scar told me about the child sacrifices held there and that he is powerless against the council. They worship El Diablo who requires blood sacrifice. I told him about Christ and how he will crush the head of the snake that is El Diablo just as prophecy says. I would have many talks about the plan of God and Christ and how El Diablo will be defeated, and that God would not require that type of sacrifice.

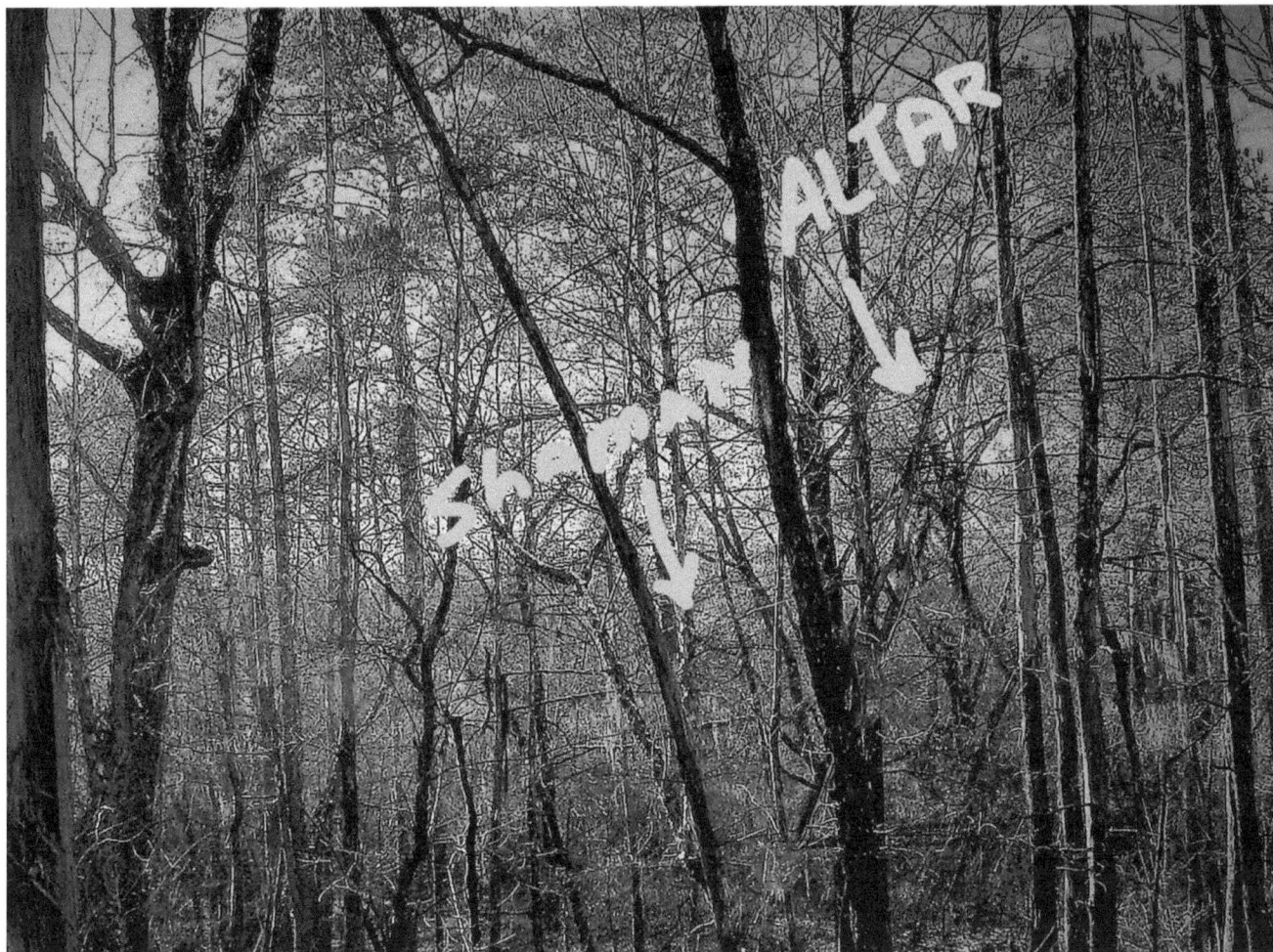

Scar told me that members of the council have been to my yard and that they were told to watch me closely as not many humans know about them. I kept this in mind while looking through my photos. One day I found that a Bigfoot that was in a picture from Fish Creek was the same individual who I saw in my front yard.

The photo from Fish Creek was in my 1ˢᵗ book and was taken in 16degree weather and the Bigfoots were ice fishing and putting their catch in woven fish baskets made from reeds. This photo was filtered with a mercury filter which made them more visible.

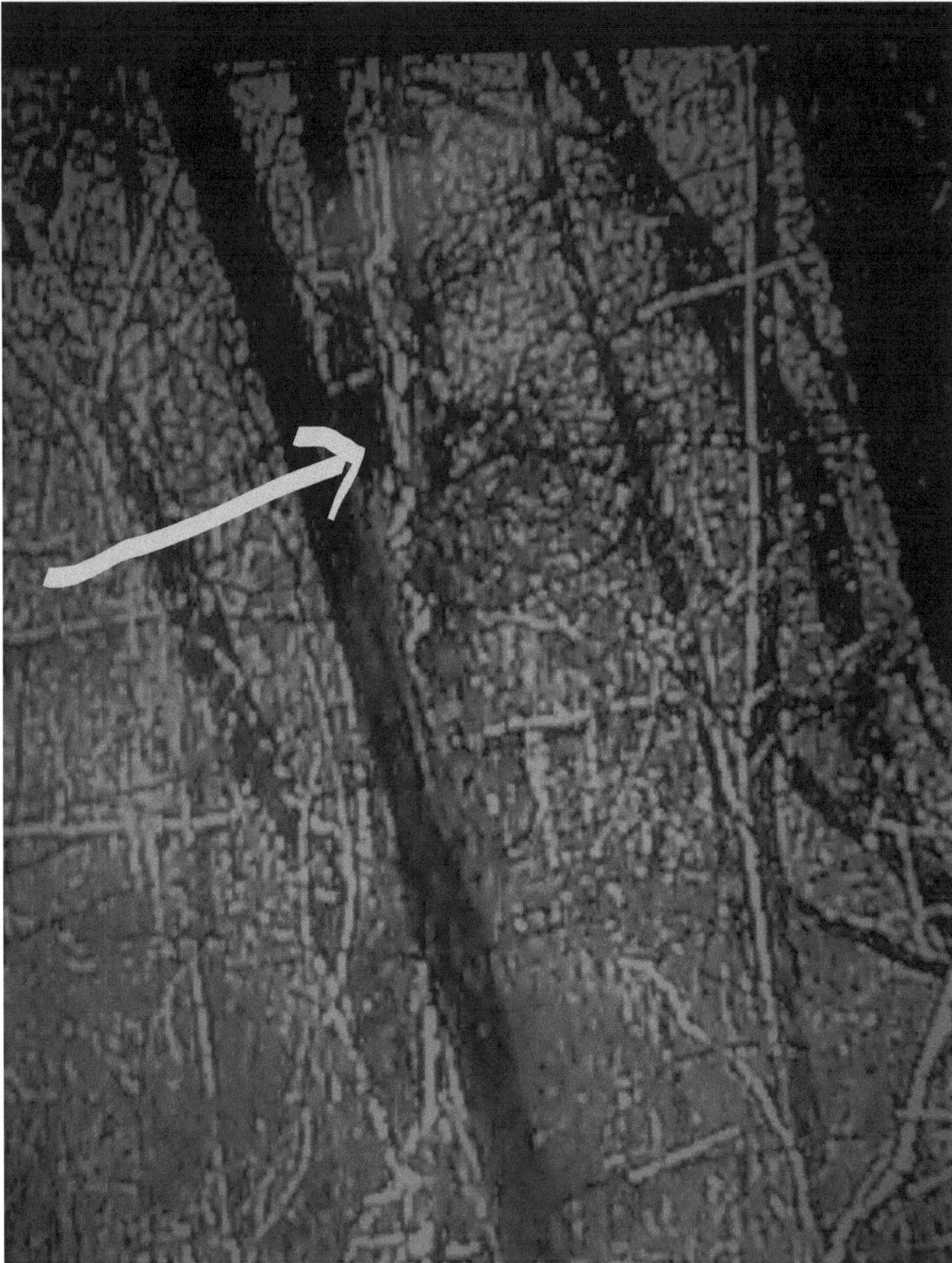

A picture of the Shaman's Crooked snake staff which is multi-colored.

Well! I am being investigated by the Mookwarruh! They seem organized, and they are watching my comings and goings. I have been talking to them telling them my words are like iron; that my words are true. I tell them that I will never fail them and that I am their friend. The Mookwarruh have about 1,000 in their population and form a theocracy in their local region, as it is ruled by a council of Priests.

Chapter 3

The Nocona Clan (wandering) of Upper Fish Creek and Panther Bayou of the Crooked Snake Tribe

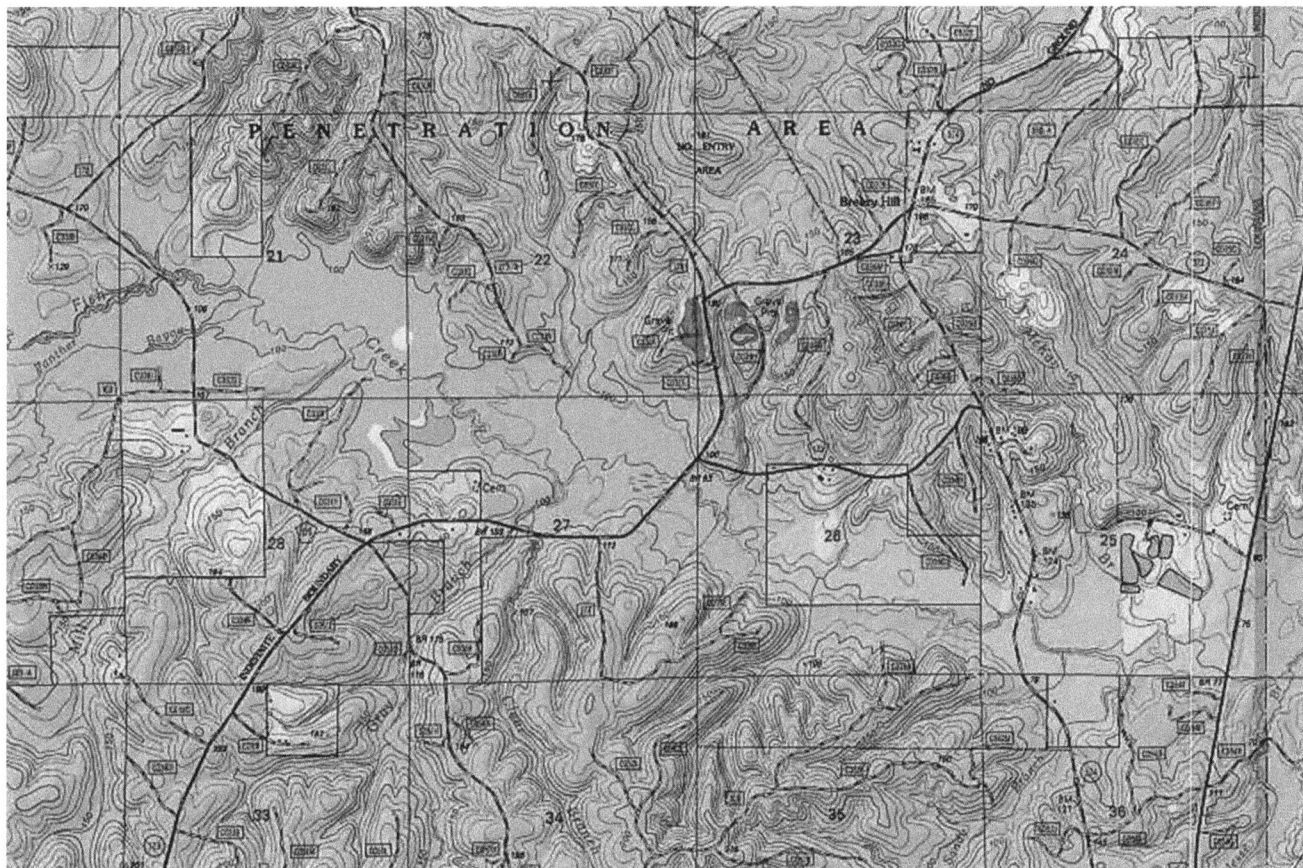

The word Nocona means wandering in Comanche and in Bigfoot. They got this name because they wander the many tributaries and valleys of Fish Creek. The clan is ruled by Esa Habbe which means wolf. There are about 400 in their group. All this information is what I learned from my talks with Scar.

Recently my ex-wife and I rode through a portion of Kisatchie National Forest. The road we were on crosses a valley that has a tributary stream that feeds into Fish Creek about a mile away. We got out of the car and stood on the bridge and called out to the Bigfoots. I told them my name and told them that I was their friend. Then my ex-wife took over talking to them and they started poking their heads up and poking around trees. We got some nice pictures. It is a beautiful little valley, a true little paradise.

They are so cute, and not quite sure about me. Then my ex-wife saved the day and spoke up.

This one was taken by me. The Bigfoots are in the picture, but they are hiding.

Anita took this picture, and some are making themselves more visible for her. I may have to take her with me more often. Besides she called me and told me she enjoyed the outing.

There are two bigfoots that are visible. One down on the ground in the center of the picture and one up in the tree to the right. Besides that, it is a beautiful picture and a true representation of the wilds of Louisiana.

Heads poking up through the grass.

A Baby on the right at the first bush. Two larger ones midway between two trees, and others in the background near the spring wellhead.

I called out for Esa Habbe and a 14foot Bigfoot stood up. He was a silverback and had the look of a leader. I spoke to him for a while and told him of my friends Brutus and Scar. I said Hi Tai! That means "Hi, friend" in Comanche.

Look in the top center of this picture.

They are getting closer and closer. Anita is over there cooing at them. We may have to leave soon!

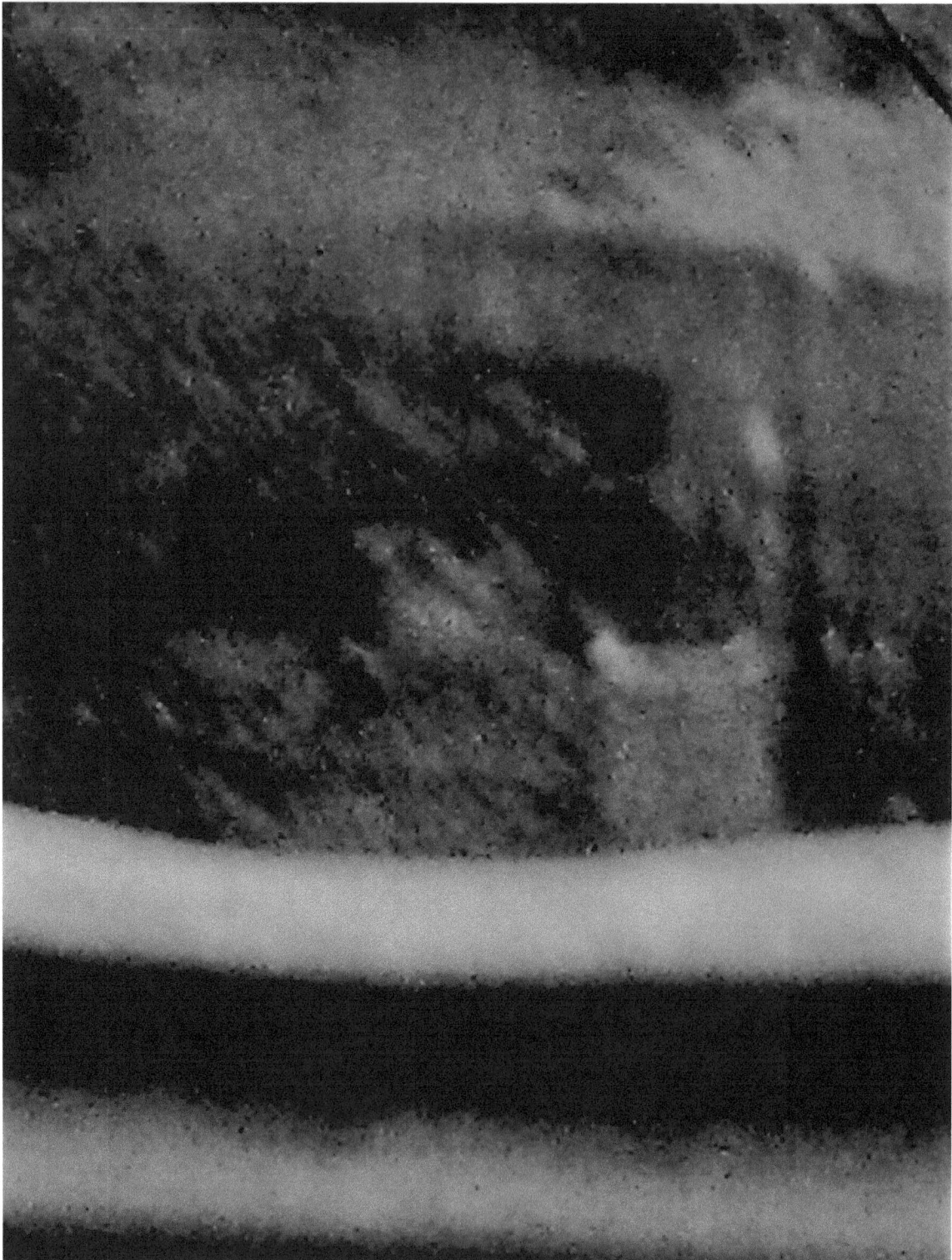

Here a bigfoot mother and children come up to the car at the foot of the bridge, just below the railing and ask for a treat. Here she is with some cookies we gave them. It's just too much isn't it? Look at the smile on the mother's face. It tells all doesn't it?

Well, we made it back to my house, to my friends, Scar and his clan, it my yard. This is Squatchland! Wow!

They like piling up and cuddling each other.

Same spot a few minutes later.

Night, night guys. See you in the morning.

In my 1st book, *Squatchland, The Mystery of the Iatt Lake Monster-Revealed*, I identified 4 different types of what I call Bigfoot as a general term. The Bigfoots, 12-20 ft, tall, the Sasquatches, 8 to 9 ft. tall, which I identified as a pre-homo sapiens man as he looks human, makes tools, rope, and weapons, then the skunk apes 6-7.5 ft. tall, and lastly unknown bi-peds varying in size and shape. Now I have identified another race with the help of my friend Scar. After looking at some pictures that I showed him he told me about a clan of Bigfoots called the No Meat Eaters. This picture was in my 1st book. At first, I thought this was a juvenile Bigfoot (big sis) taking care of her sisters and brothers. Scar told me that this female was an adult. They are much smaller than the meat eaters.

I went back and zoomed in and found others in my pictures that match the size of the one in my original picture. Here is the original picture.

Louisiana is indeed a ***Sportsman's Paradise,*** the nickname for Louisiana. It is also a paradise for many creatures as well as Bigfoots. I believe this may be the most beautiful picture I have ever taken, and I have visited 40 states. Look at that cute little Bigfoot on the right trying to stay still. Below I cropped these pictures out of this picture.

She has babies all around her and her male looks to be to the right. Here he is.

And there are others in the swamp.

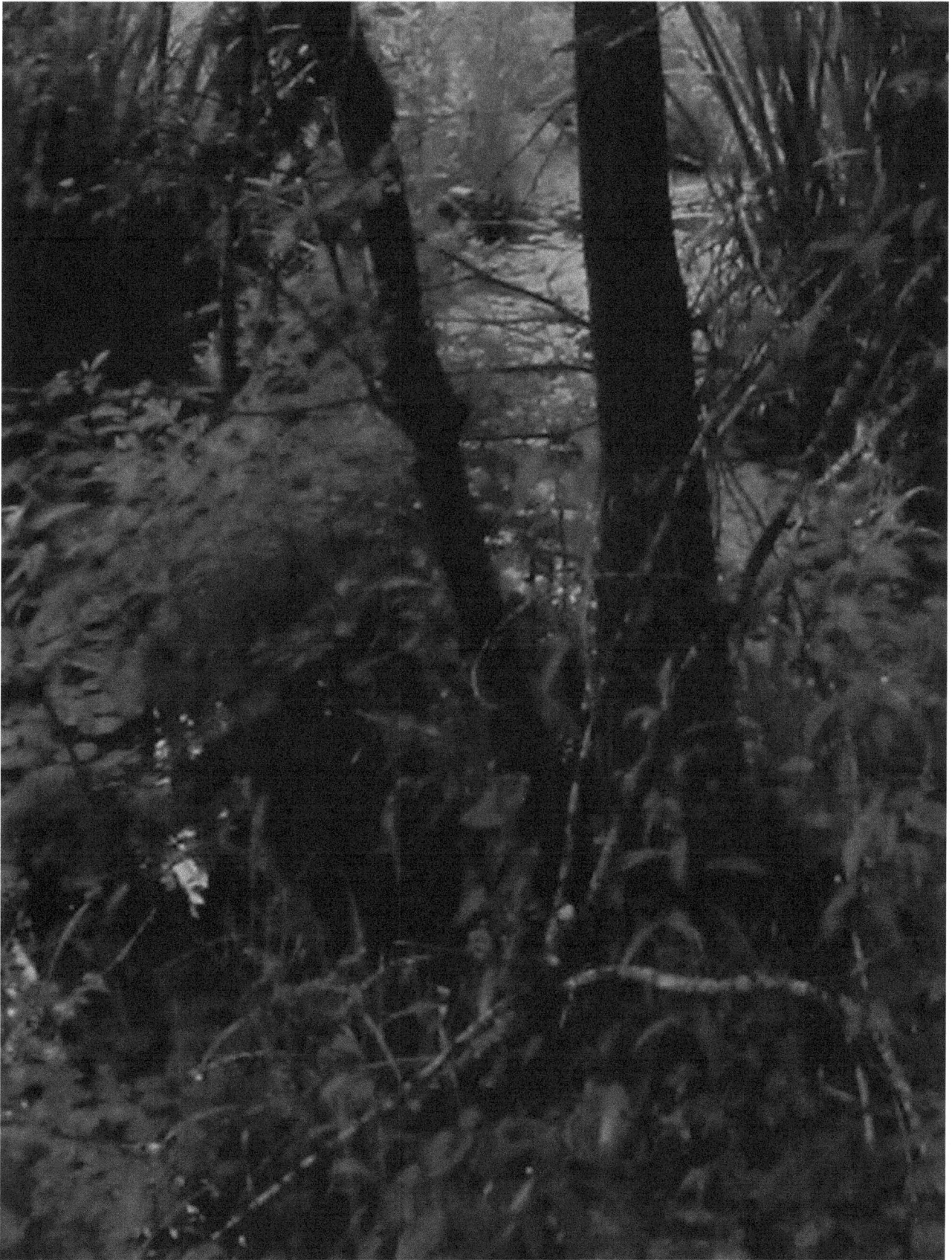

There are some on the top right and left as well as in the middle and a few babies scattered around. They are much smaller, not violent, and at peace with nature.

Clear Creek. Bigfoots in the center of this picture.

Cropped out of the center of the previous picture. He looks wild.

One last picture of clear creek.

What a paradise. Clear, clean flowing water damned by beavers, creating a backwater or swamp; a living swamp, full of life. Bigfoots only drink clean, clear water, and they are going to take their pick of where they live, so you know that wherever they choose to live, it will provide everything they need. Look top center at the grey one's face.

This is a group of Sasquatches living at Clear creek with the Tekwapi. The big male towers over the others. You can bet the Tekwapi pose no threat to him.

Chapter 5

Clan of the Lance (Spear) of the Crooked Snake Tribe of Dartigo Creek Valley

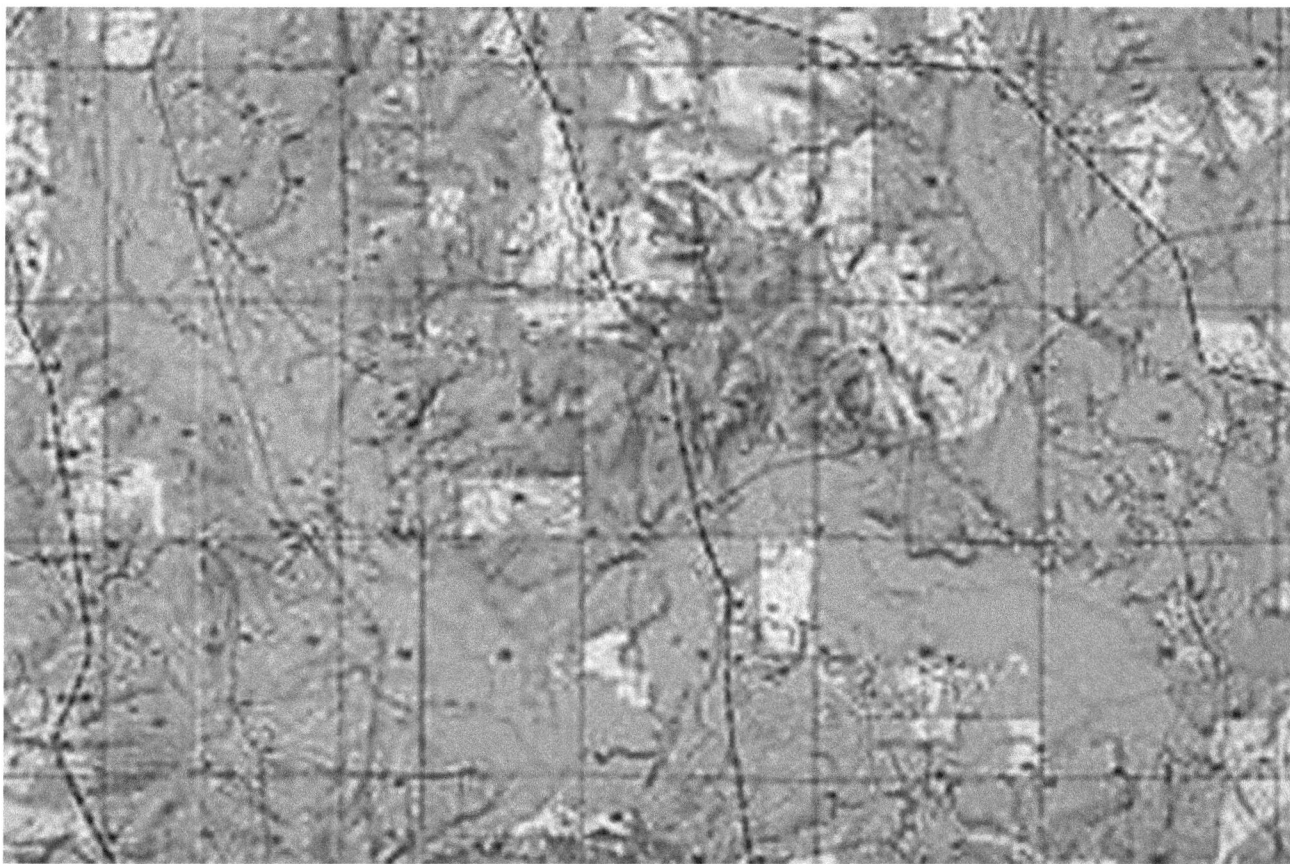

The woods are so tall and thick that most of the creeks and swamp are hidden from view from satellite so I drew in the creeks with a highlighter pen.

I realize that this map does not help a lot and that there are few landmarks, and that is good. For one thing it is literally out in the middle of nowhere. Secondly, I don't want to help anyone find it as it is a garden of Eden, and a refuge for a very large population of Bigfoots of all forms. Their number is around 2000. It is also where I first encountered these creatures and began to document, photograph, and worked on developing a relationship with a large Sasquatch who I named Brutus. Brutus and I have never sat down and talked but we would knock to each other and were friendly to each other. I lived at Dartigo for a little over a year across from a large swamp that had creeks feeding it. Damned by beavers a mile wide, water falls over the damn, forming one large creek heading on to Lake Iatt in The Kisatchie National Forest. There was a spring next to the swamp that was built into a wellhead. Bigfoots would come to drink several times a day. When Brutus and his family would come to drink, he would give me a knock. I would yell hi back. The well was 80 yards or more away. I drank from the well many times and the water was clean. I would hear noises at night such as hogs squealing and running as if being herded, then clubbing and squealing, then no sound. I would hear wood knocks at night as if they were coordinated. They hunted and ate wild hogs and deer and ate many wild blueberries when in season. Dartigo Valley remains a study area for me and I expect to sit down with Brutus one day. Brutus is 8-foot-tall, 600-700 pounds, and has a war club like a Huron Indian war club. His spear is 10-foot-tall with a sharp stone spear tip and the shaft is well worked smooth and round and straight. Sasquatches form a warrior class amongst all the "Bigfoots", and they are feared by all. Most of the bigfoots are telepathic and communicate telepathically with each other and lack communication skills with humans, however the Sasquatches are the most communicative.

This footprint was found near the well.

This is a picture of Brutus standing at the corner of the abandoned house across the street from my rented shotgun Cajun style tin roofed house with a front porch. Bigfoots are in the trees, on the roof, and in the woods. Brutus is their King.

A close- up of Brutus, with spear and club.

The club dangles from a rope or twine from his neck. It bobs up and down as he runs. A baby jumped off his back on to the side of the house and is holding on to the window frame. They look so much more human than the others and can be heard speaking to each other the way humans would, they may be telepaths but that is not their primary mode of communication. They are the most warlike of all the Bigfoots and are to be feared. They can hold their own against a giant Bigfoot because of their skills with weapons. Weapons are their equalizers and they have dominion over the rest of the creatures. The Sasquatches are a form of early man, a caveman. Something we were told was extinct many years ago.

My best picture to date of a Sasquatch is my first picture. First, I found this footprint filling up with water. Then I raised up and caught this female and child out in the open. She is standing in 4 feet of water.

I rose up and took this picture.

I then took this one.

David T. Hollis 2/4/17

Dartigo Swamp

Out of this picture I cropped out this female Sasquatch with baby. Bigfoots are all around her.

The photo was published on BFRO website and listed as a sighting in Grant Parish, La. Dartigo is a major feast site as well as a sacrificial worship area. They have a ruling council of elders or priests, but they share power with the Sasquatches and Brutus their King. They act as advisors and influencers to Brutus, whose Bigfoot name is Mo Cho Rook, which means the cruelest one of all.

 I decided to take a canoe up stream to see if I could get close to what I believe is an altar stone on an island in the middle of the swamp by taking an old creek run to the oxbow.

Bigfoots were lining the bank the entire way. You cannot make a move in these woods without being seen. I am trying to get close to the sacrificial island, but I fear I will be forced back. There could be prima facia evidence of Bigfoot on this island. I took this picture from my first book showing a female carrying a skull of her dead husband around.

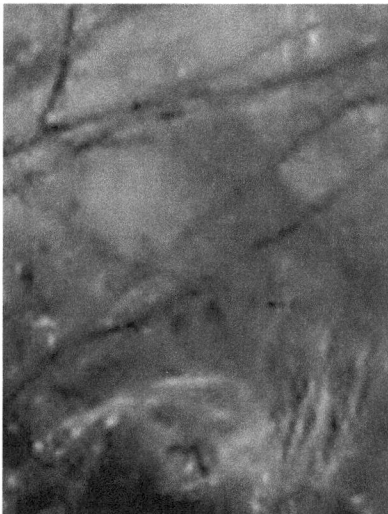

As I approached the sacrificial island, I had large sticks, rocks, and debris thrown at me. I backed up very quickly.

There is a delta triangle shaped stone that is hollow like an arch. There are many guards on the island and will not allow approach. Let's look at another view.

I know these pictures are not perfect. I am trying to zoom in on the triangle stone which leaves everything else blurry.

Another view from the creek after I pulled my canoe into shore.

The island in the background has many Bigfoots guarding it. They followed me all the way to my car. I waived and told them I was sorry for going where I should not have gone.

They are on the island with a very large one in the middle of the picture. Notice some of them are on this side of the creek, out of the woods and out of cover. It still amazes me that other folks don't see them like I do. They must think I am special and allow me to see them. Most folks don't even know about them, and they like it that way.

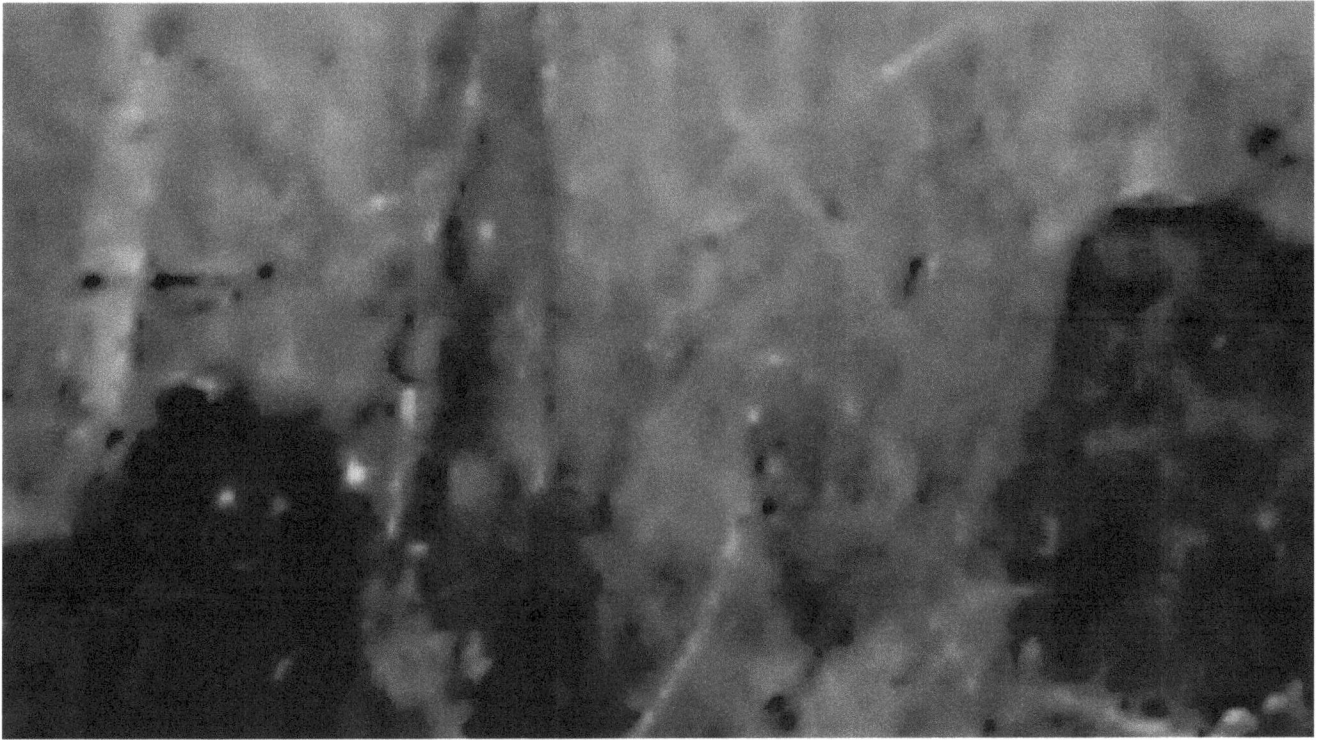

One last look, Bigfoots on the bank.

Look at the noses on these two. One has their hair in corn rolls or pigtails.

This is a deer run. They herd the deer into this swamp through the clearing and when the depth reaches 5 foot, and the deer must swim causing them to slow down. Then Bigfoots from either side jump them. I have found many deer tracks headed into the swamp right here. I see some shapes in the brush.

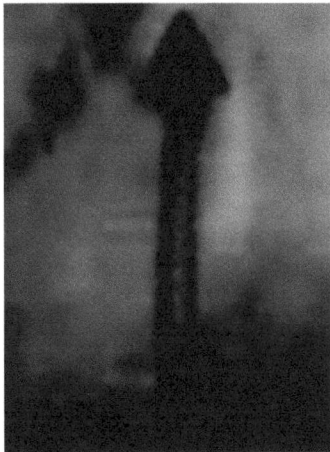
Brutus' spear

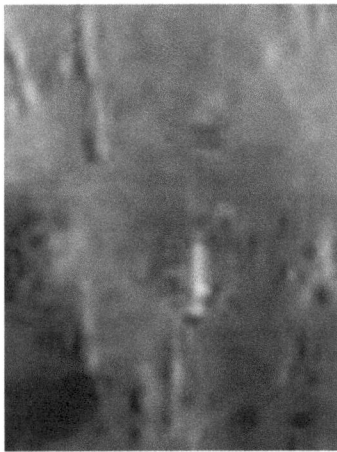
A reed whistle in the mouth of this one

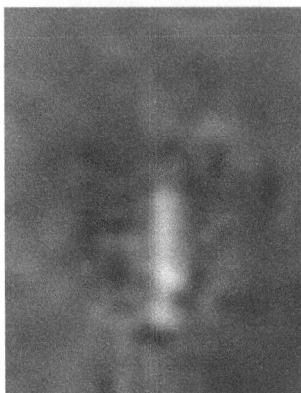

A close- up of the reed whistle.

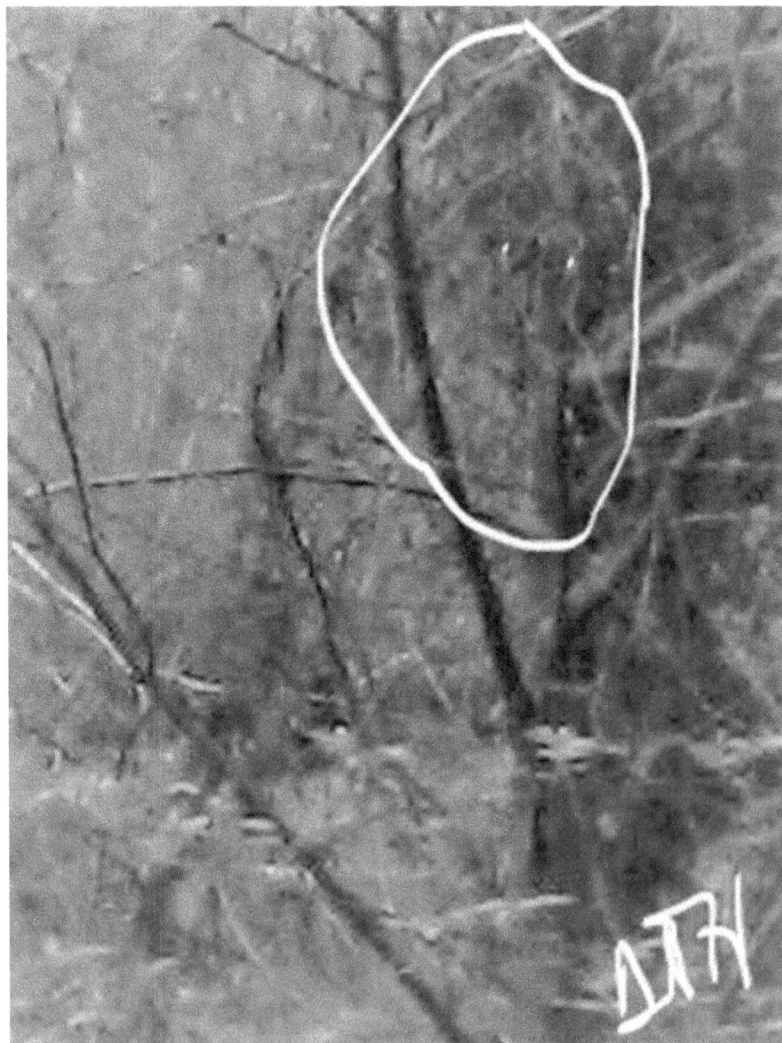

This Sasquatch is "Grey Wolf" as his hair is grey. He has a club shaped a lot like a bowling pin dangling from a twine around his neck and around the neck of the club. He can run while the club dangles leaving his hands available for other things. The bottom picture is enhanced for context. Can you see the twine around the neck of his club? Grey Wolf is a General for Mo Cho Rook. Here he is with his troop.

He is directly in the center of this picture.

The picture above are Bigfoots spearfishing and using fish baskets to keep their fish. They are in icy waters and the fish are moving slowly so they are easy to spear. A ray of light is on the tree that is holding a fish basket made of reeds with a flip top lid. You can see the weave on the basket. Also, you can see ice floating down stream, they must have broken up the ice to fish.

Below a close- up of the fish basket in black and white. See Bigfoots?

These Bigfoots are in an area that they opened in a thicket to drive hogs toward an ambush spot I call the Hog chute.

The "Hog Chute" where Bigfoots ambush hogs with clubs and spears. This is just some of the ways that Bigfoots use the terrain and weapons and tactics used to hunt their game.

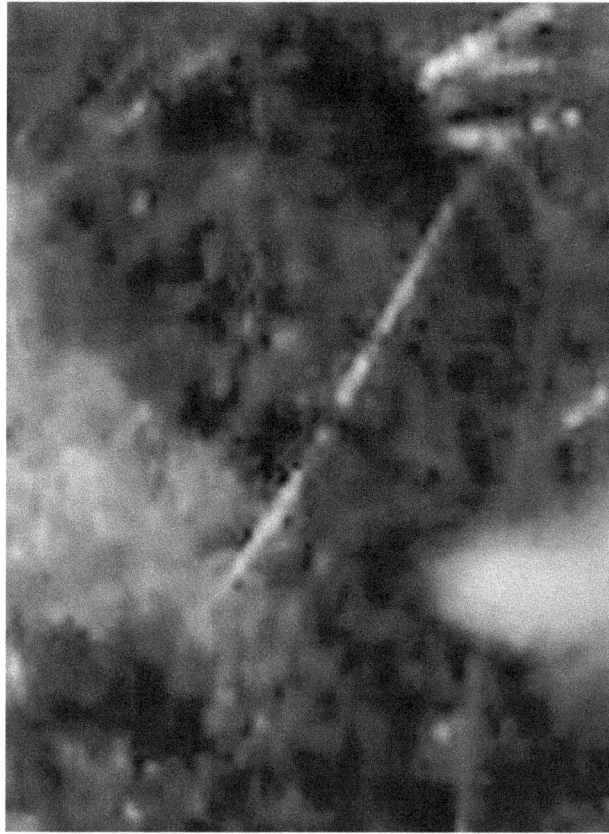

This Bigfoot has a fur around his neck to keep warm. He is also carrying a hog he has killed.

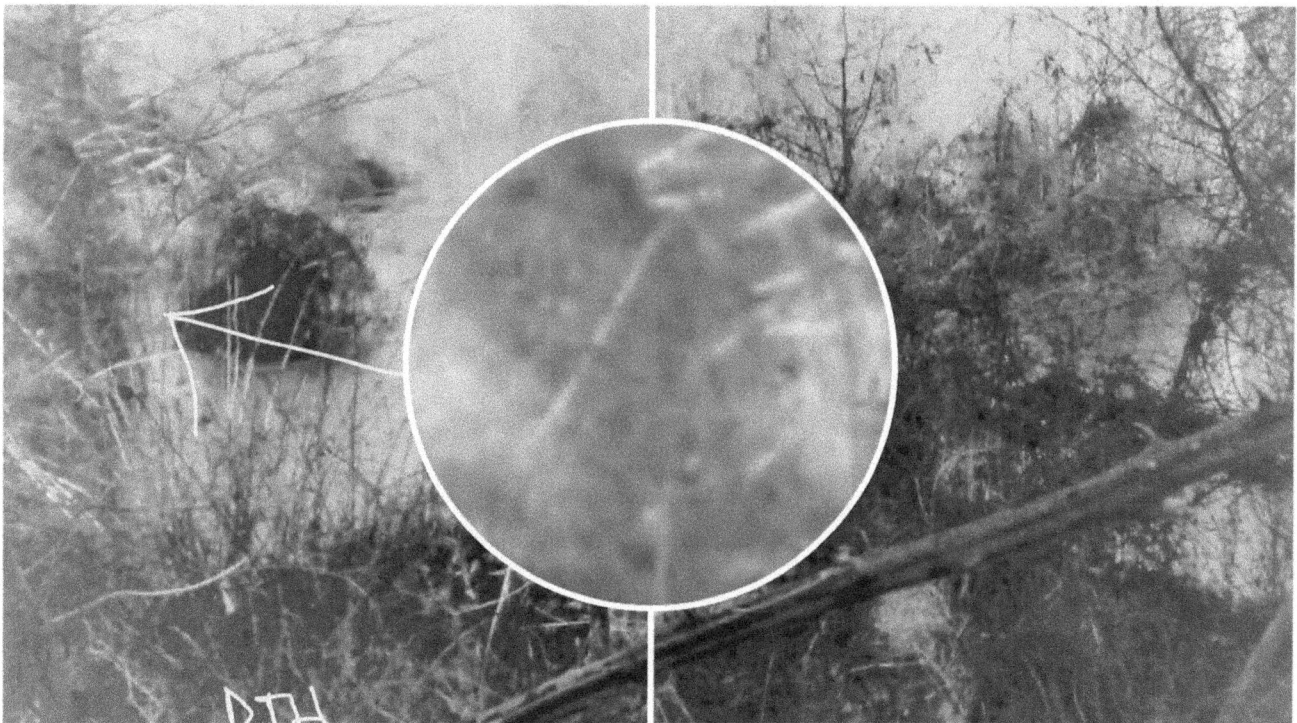

Bigfoots have large families; therefore, they must be successful at hunting to provide for their family. Bigfoots have thrived as they are filling the role that other apex predators once filled.

Chapter 7

8- foot Trails and Arches.

One way to find Bigfoots is to look for eight- foot trails and arches. What I mean by that is when you see a wide trail, eight- foot wide and eight -foot tall or more, it may be frequently used by these creatures. Bigfoots do not like to get hit in the face by branches on their hi-ways that I call eight-foot trails. These trails lead to nurseries, blueberry patches, deer trails, hog wallows, and springs with clean, clear water. These trails lead to streams, creeks, and swamps and from one clan to another. An eight-foot trail with arch here, straight ahead.

What is down this trail you may ask? This is not evidence of anything some may say. However, this is what I found:

See this mother with her child in front of her? There are other adults behind her. A canine tooth shows from her mouth.

Behind and to the right of the arch is a mass of bigfoots. I waived, told them hi, and told them their babies were pretty and backed out of there. This is near Hall Hollow.

Let's look down some other trails.

This is a perfect example of an eight-foot trail. There are huge Bigfoots straight ahead. My doctor told me I need to walk 5000 steps per day and this trail looks very nice to walk. A lot of traffic wears down this trail as it almost looks to be mowed. So, let's go down the trail. I must psyche myself up for this.

Huge Bigfoots ahead!

I told them my doctor wants me to walk more and I hope they don't mind me coming through. Although these Bigfoots are of the Adecca clan and Scar is their Chief, I do not know them. I tell them Tai, Tai, which means Friend! I keep going and see this.

The trail is narrowing, and this guy is on the trail and he is not moving. The elevation drops more than one hundred feet just ahead, so to save face I stop and do my stretches and I tell this Bigfoot that that is as far as I want to go. I tell him bye and turn around and leave. Who knows, it could be a girl. Curious I guess; maybe I missed out on an opportunity to meet this Bigfoot. See the trail off to the right on the way back.

Bigfoots in the woods on the way back, all the way back. See the arch?

Here are Bigfoots making an arch. They are in the top of these trees and bending them down. I walk down this trail not noticing this until later when examining my pictures. I saw a trail and an arch and walked on.

I went a little farther and ran into this scene. I stopped and turned around when I saw this.

They look a little busy.

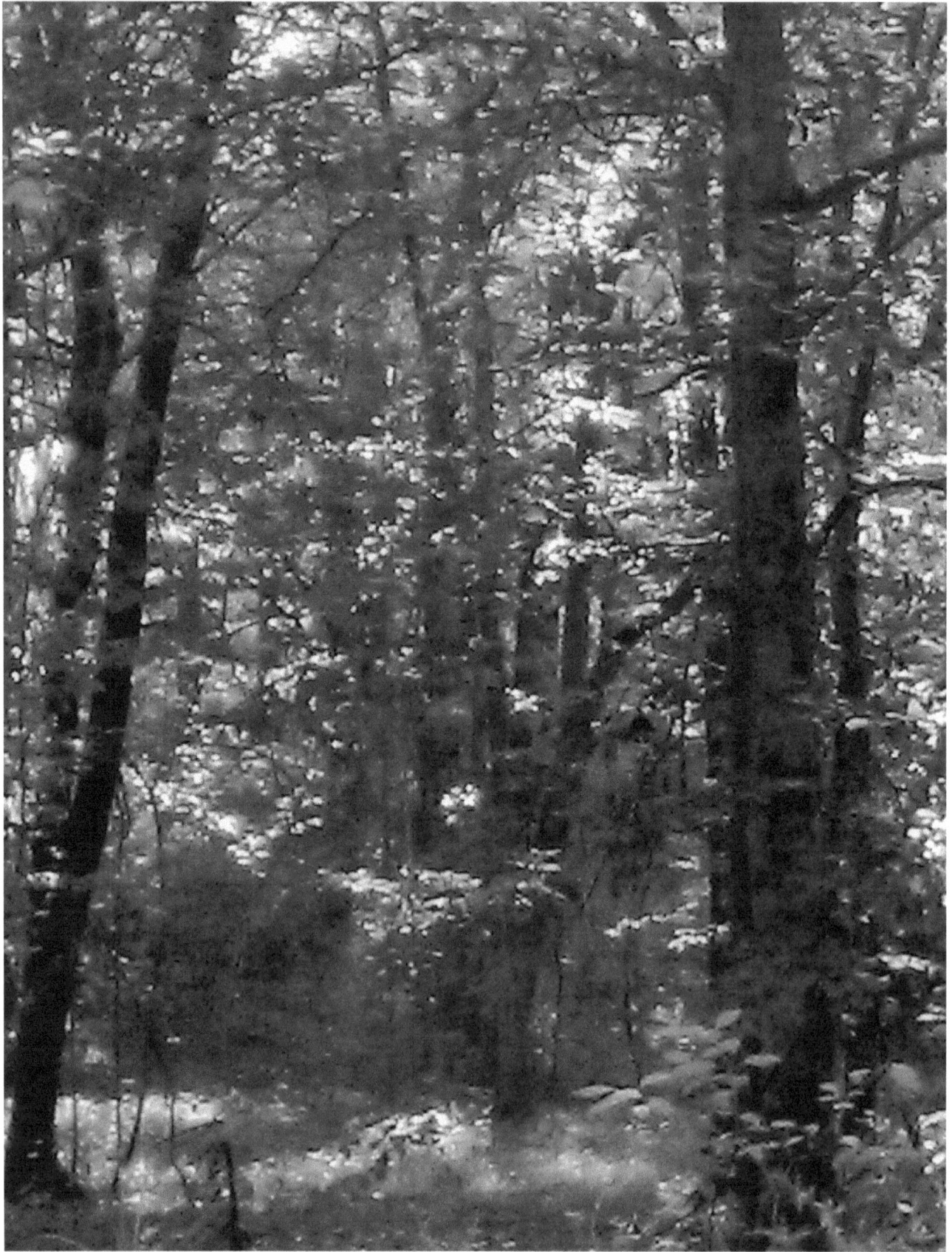

Here is another eight-foot trail with a very human looking sasquatch sitting on the trail. I ask him if I can pass and he grunts and moves off in the brush. I must be nuts.

Let's get a better look at this Sasquatch.

With her male behind her and her children around her they form a "clutch"" or "pod". They let me pass. I want to go down this trail to see where it leads as there is a change in elevation. I soon find their little paradise that they have all to themselves.

Bigfoots in the brush up and down the trail.

Bigfoot Paradise! There is a cave just ahead with Bigfoots at the entrance. Also, the cliff has a couple of slides. One in the center of the picture has several Bigfoots standing there. Game comes to drink here and get ambushed daily.

Several Bigfoots lay in wait for game to come drink. There are large faces in the brush.

This trail is at Dartigo Creek Valley.

An eight-foot trail, complete with arch, and Bigfoots on either side of the trail. I have spent a lot of time with these guys and they do not hide anymore. Once through the arch you can go left to the hog chute or go right to the swamp and the deer run. Straight ahead is the hog wallow.

They lie in wait for hogs to come in. Many Bigfoots are just inside the wood line.

Bigfoots at the water's edge.

Bigfoots near the mouth of the creek before it joins the small lake I found.

On the way out, I went up the creek and stood on a bluff overlooking the creek and the small lake behind it. Bigfoots are in the woods.

Then I ran into these guys.

As you can see, going down arched trails can be very interesting!

I woke up one morning and went out to get the mail and as soon as I stepped outside, I heard a familiar knock. It was not a warning but a greeting. I recognized the sound and frequency of the knock as Brutus, the King of Dartigo Swamp and Leader of the Clan of the Lance. When I moved back to Central Louisiana, I moved to Dartigo as my house on the other side of the parish was rented. When my home became available, I moved and told Brutus where I was moving and invited him and his group to come see me sometime. I went over and sat about ten feet from him as we were never that close, and our friendship was more based on mutual respect rather than friendship. He told me that they were going to the fall feast at Fish Creek and heard where I was and came by. I told him I was so glad to see him. I told him that I was honored to have him come by. Brutus' name in Sasquatch is Mo Cho Rook. His name means the cruelest one of all. He is a fierce King and has a war club, and a spear or lance that is ten-foot tall. He uses rope or twine and uses furs to keep warm. The Sasquatches or more human, and more able to make tools and weapons. The Sasquatches take advantage of their intellect and special abilities and rule over the other varieties with an iron hand. I have learned to show him respect but not gravel in his presence. He likes how I handle him and likes how I stand up for myself. I will bow to him but not on bended knee like the others. He likes this because he likes to think he is an equal to me or that he is in my league. He let me take a picture of him which is great as it is only my second one of him. I went in and got some tobacco and beef jerky. We sat and ate and smoked and talked for a while. This is the most communication I have ever gotten out of him. He rules over two thousand Bigfoots, Sasquatches, and Skunk Apes, and hybrids. His rule is tenuous at best. He could not be seen communicating so closely with me at Dartigo because he has much competition and others vying for supremacy. His reputation comes from ruling with an iron hand. The Sasquatches like humans the least, but they emulate humans and learn from them. They also have dominion over all living things just like the humans. They reason, contemplate, make and use complex tools and weapons. Their language is complex with some seven hundred words. Some words are Sasquatch, and some are Comanche, Apache, Sioux, Chippewa, English and Mexican.   Brutus has heard about my relationship with Scar and he has wanted to be closer to me, so he decided to leave the group with only his immediate family to drop by on the way to the feast.

I told Brutus that I was honored that he came by and that these Bigfoots over here do not communicate very much. He told me that a lot of them are telepaths, so they don't use clubs to do wood knocks. He said if I hear a wood knock it is usually a Sasquatch and there aren't many of them in this area.

This is the scene as I approached. Brutus and family are sitting. He has his arm around her. His Guard stands behind him. His children are around the couple. I approach with care and respect and bow to him to show respect for the King. Just a little bow however.

Brutus (Mo Cho Rook) the Sasquatch sitting next to his wife and his children sitting all around them. He is King of the Tribe of the Crooked Snake. I just must pinch myself! This is just too good to be true. God has allowed this. There just cannot be any other answer. Most people are not going to believe all of this. However, it is real! Who can get this close to Sasquatch and they keep sitting? Let's look at this again.

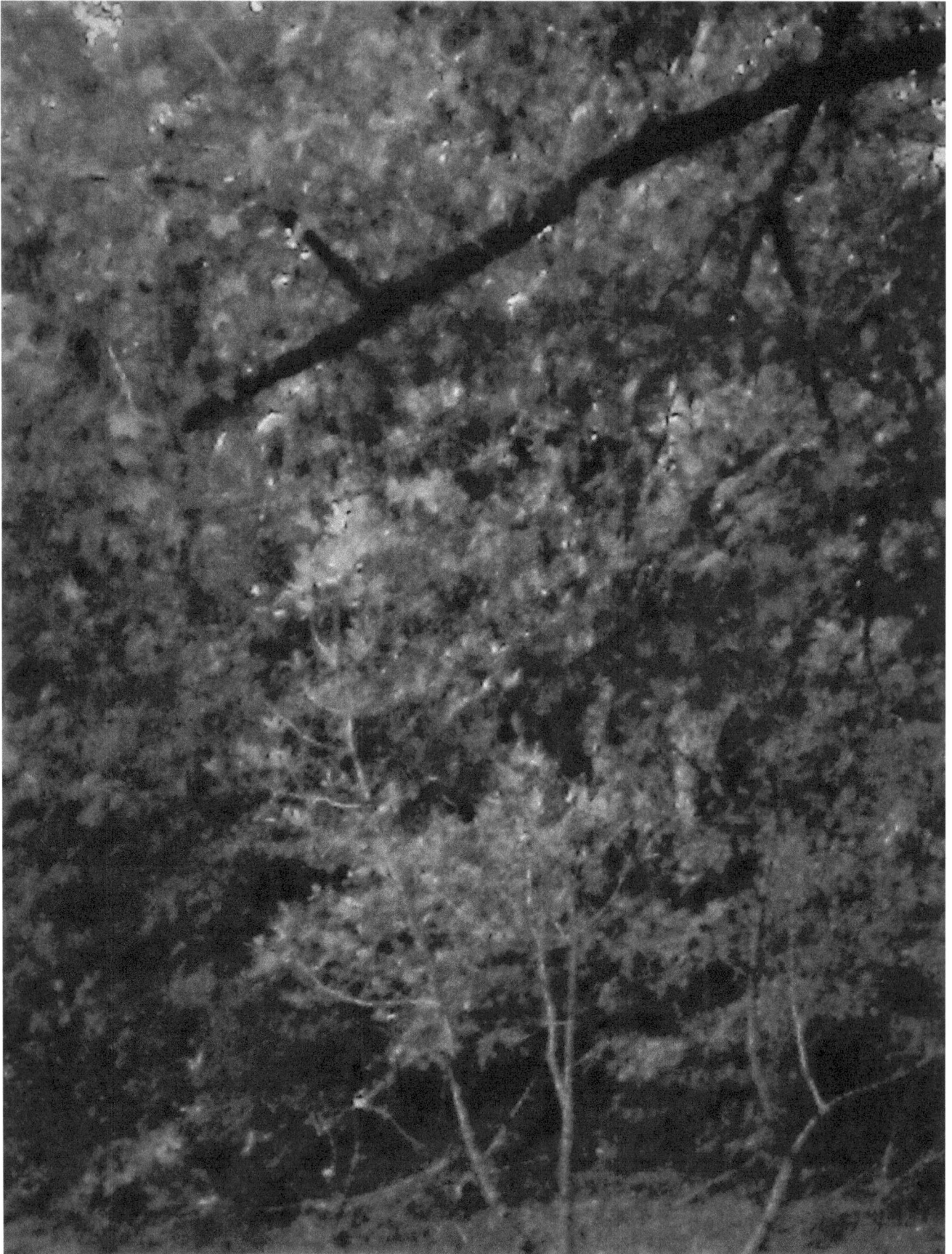

I took this when I left.

Others in the presence of their King. A Train is behind them.

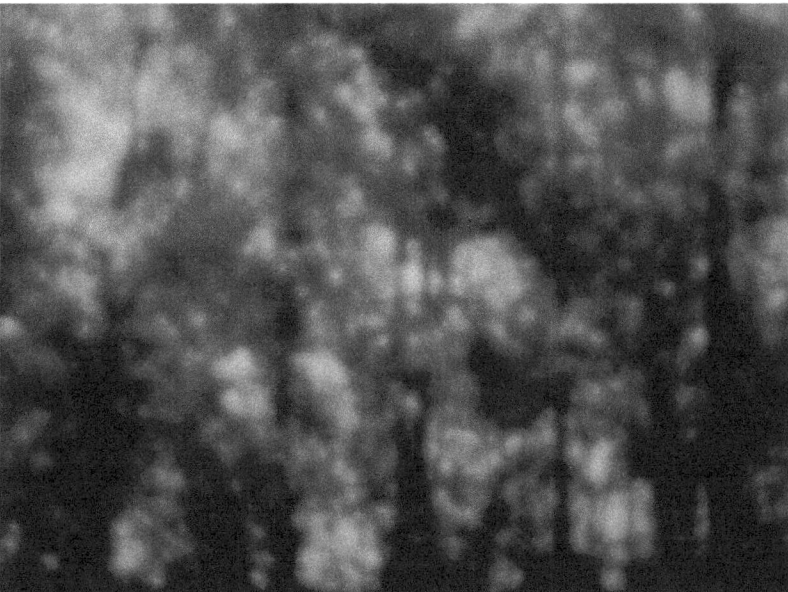

Some even painted their faces getting ready for their feast.

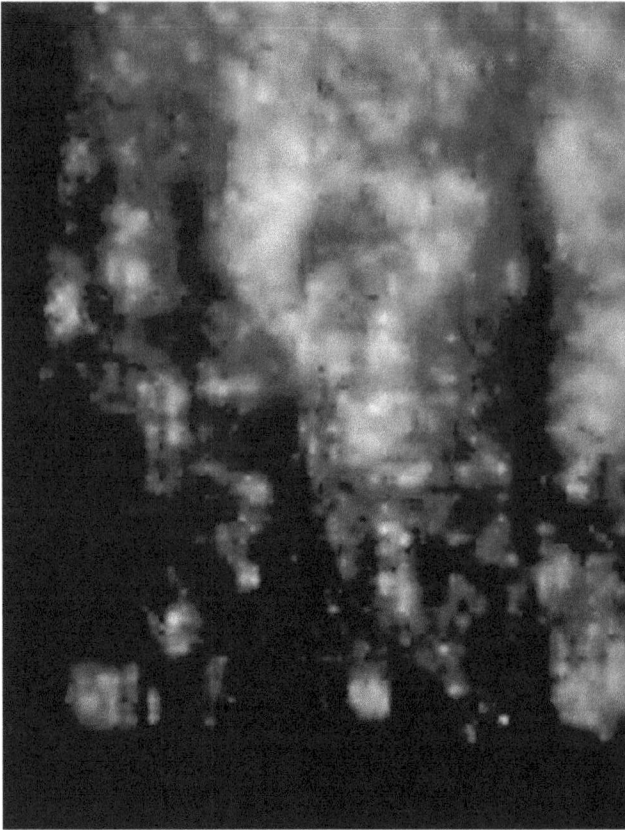

They all seemed happy and excited. They would all travel together about four miles from here with their King and family with them!

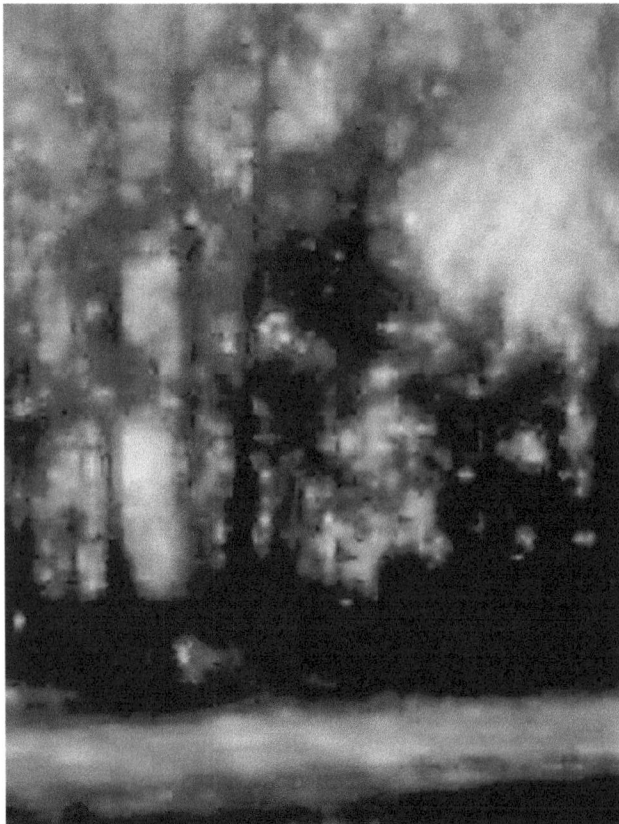

This was a very good day with all of them being so visible as their King felt good about meeting with me so that made it ok for me to "see" them also.

More feast goers gathering to travel together to their feast.

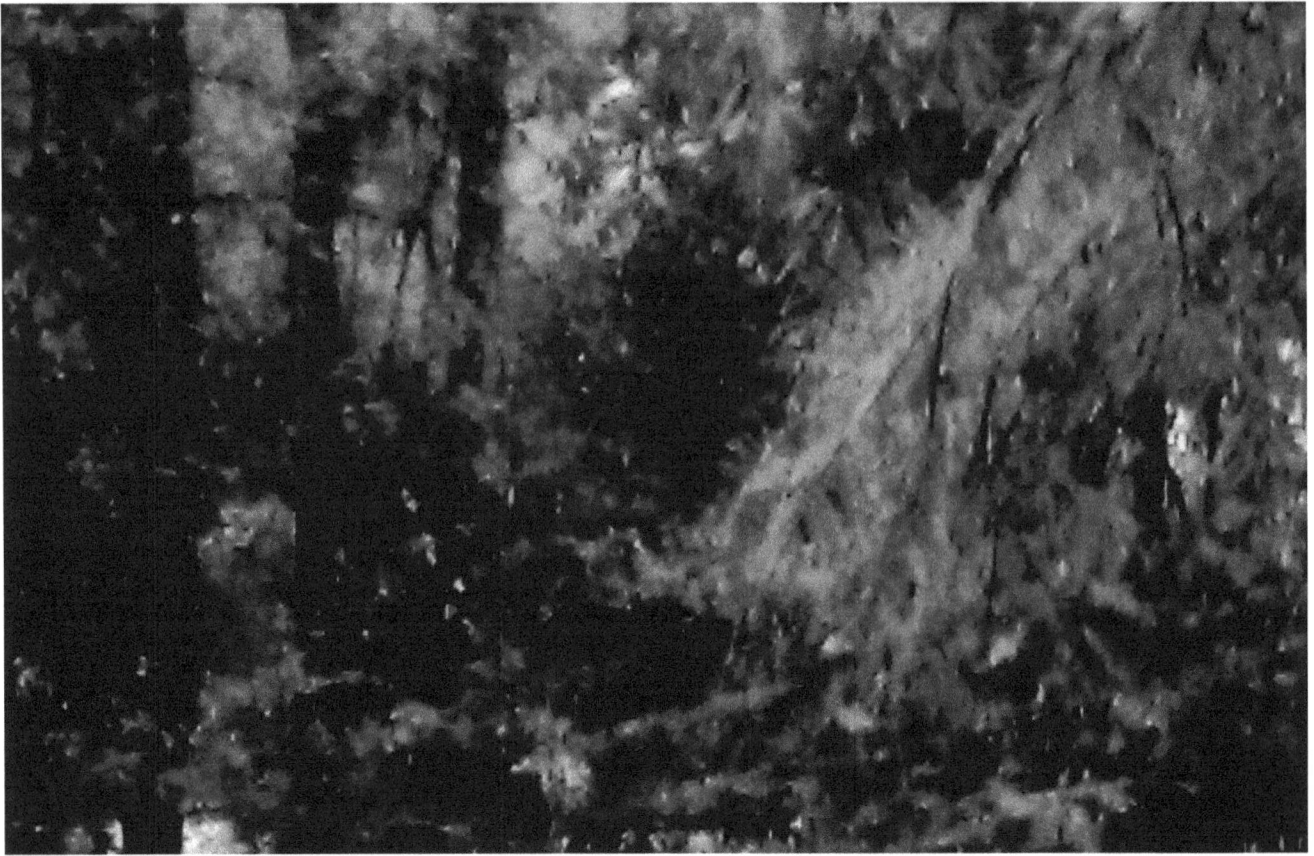

This is all going on in my yard! Can you believe it? Wow! I know there are a lot of people out there with superb technology who I am sure could get a clearer picture or could they? Would they capture the magnitude of this moment? Would they know it was happening if it was? Would Bigfoots get this close to this someone who has all this superior technology. Who could take a better picture? Some guys dress in Gilley suits and hike for days trying to sneak up on Bigfoot. I carry my cellphone and get close by making friends. Clear or not, it is hard to deny the number of "blobsquatches". The sheer number of them of all sizes is hard to deny. They don't mind me taking pictures. I call my phone my "magic eye box" that helps me see them. They are used to it.

A pecking order, the tallest first down to the smallest last.

See you later Guys!

The view from my porch before I go in. They are completely showing themselves. What a great day! The best day in many ways so far.

12/23/2019, I was sitting on my front porch and I began to film them while asking to see a baby. Well, I certainly got more than I asked for when a beautiful Sasquatch Mother came in and jumped right in front of my camera. The entire film can be found on my YouTube Channel, Squatchland-The Dartigo Creek Valley Project. It is truly one of the best pieces of evidence since the 1967 capture of Patty walking across Bluff Creek in Northern California. I showed it to famous forensic film analysist M.K. Davis and he said it was extraordinary. I named her Ashanti after the name kept coming to my mind and it did not quit until I named her that. Also I named her baby Twilight.

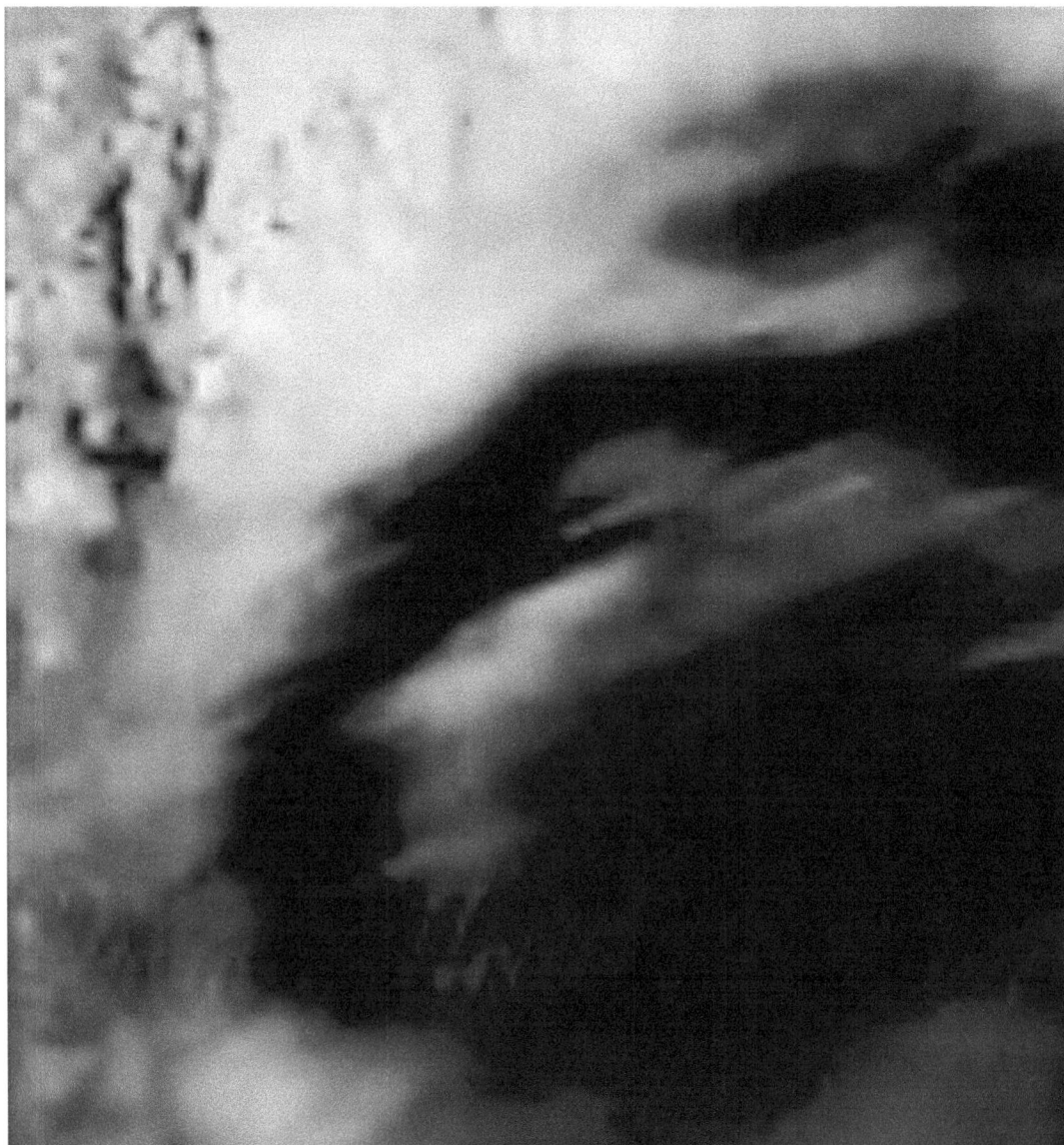

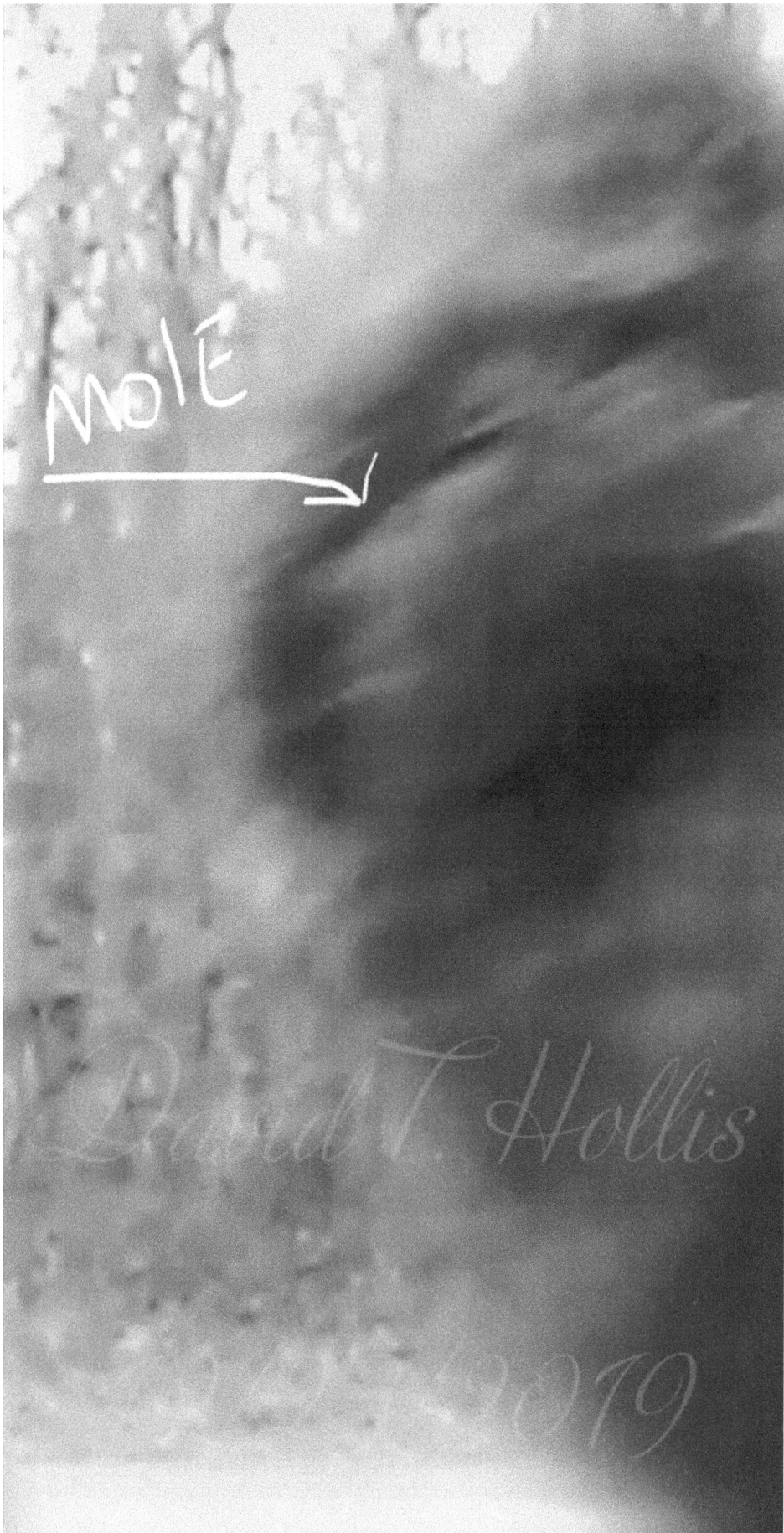

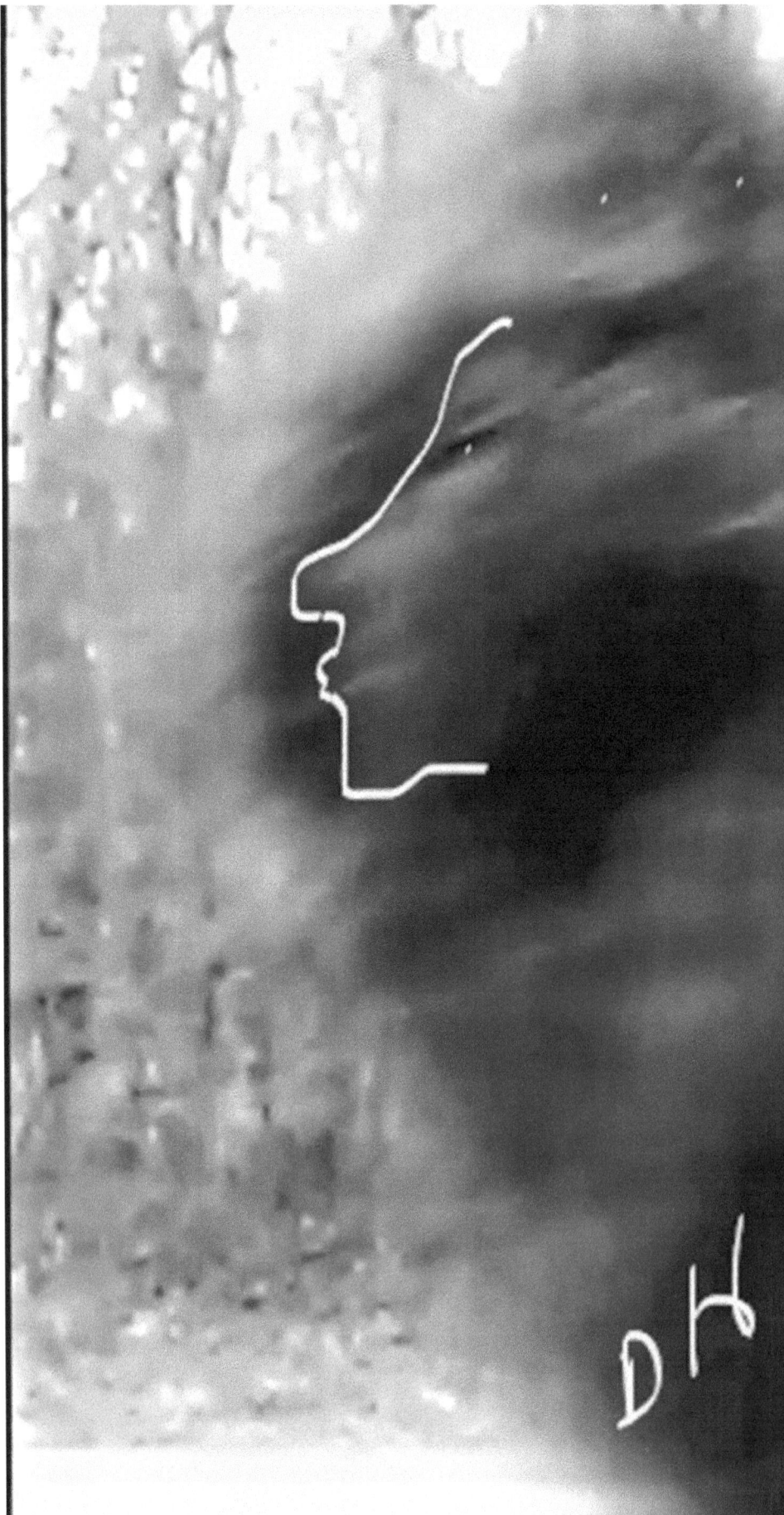

After she turned!

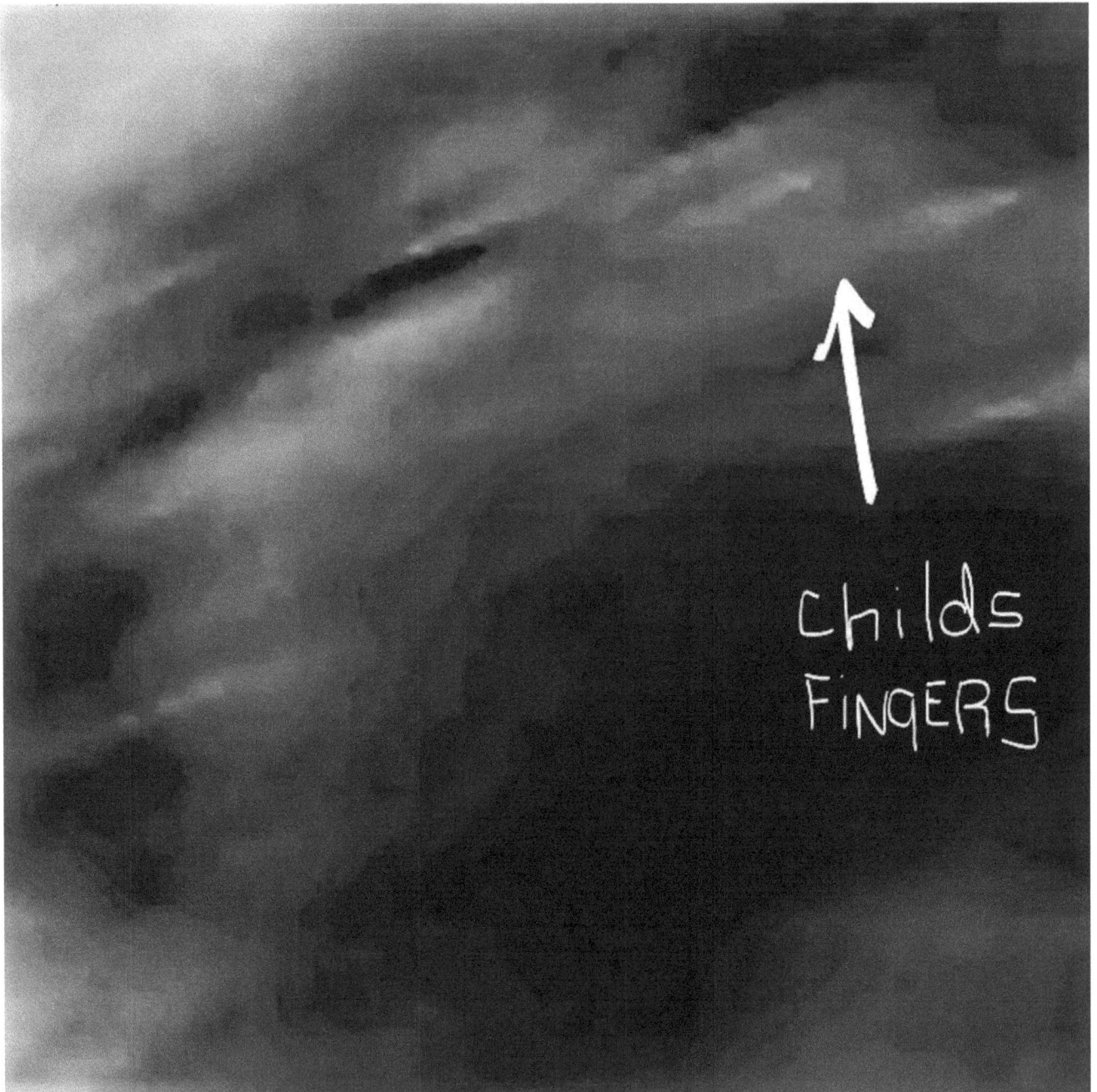

Can't fake this!

Chapter 10

The Cold Irony

On January 17th of 2018, Carter Brushardt, of Liberty, Missouri, a senior investigator with the BFRO (Bigfoot Field Research Organization) came down to check out my work and some of the areas where I have had contact with these creatures. It was the most brutal cold day I have ever experienced in Louisiana ever. I took some pictures of the snow in my yard and sent it to friends and family. Snow is a big deal here as I have only seen snow a few times in Louisiana and only a few times in my life.

I met Carter at the local Huddle House in Pineville where we talked about where we would be going and discussed the terrain and goals for our outing. We decided to go to Dartigo Creek Valley and Swamp, which is the site of my first sighting and pictures that were published on the BFRO website. It was sixteen degrees when we stepped out of the car. Along the trail Bigfoots were huddled up trying to keep warm. They did not move to hide from us as it was too cold. Here are some of the pictures from that morning.

Look to the far left, there are three, and straight ahead there are several in the distance (top right). Notice that the trail is wide and tall, an eight- foot trail. We went a little further down the trail and saw bigfoots huddled up like pods or clutches, trying to keep their babies warm.

Top Right on the bottom picture shows a male albino Bigfoot with a different female this time. I guess he is not married. Another time I caught him with this female.

We went on a little further down the trail and saw more clutches.

Even on a cold and dreary day, Louisiana is a paradise. So full of life and wonderous creatures, remote and virtually undisturbed.

I took these pictures on the way out near the spring wellhead that they drink clean water from daily.

 Carter says he did not see any Bigfoots in any of the cameras that he used. He had a Go-Pro strapped to his chest and a digital camera in his hands. He also said he did not see any Bigfoots on the digital camera that I was using as well as my cellphone. I told him that I saw them in every picture as I was taking them. It was very disappointing as it was cold, and I took him to my best spot, and I was confirming to him as I took the pictures that they were in them. However, the most ironic thing was that we did not even have to leave my house and yard. Remember me talking about the pictures I took of the snow in my yard? Looking at those pictures months later I discovered that the Bigfoots had found me, and my yard much earlier than I thought. We could have taken all the pictures of Bigfoot right here without going on such an excursion.

They sit frozen like statues with ice and snow hanging on their fur.

Some of these guys are huge!

Well, I enjoyed the outing very much and I hope Carter did also. It was a long drive for him, and I appreciate him coming.

I was looking through an old book that I bought at a book sale at a local library. The book, Louisiana's Natural Resources copywrite in 1944, which was a State of Louisiana free textbook, written by John B. Robson, Professor of Education, Northwestern State College, Natchitoches, Louisiana. In the book he shows farming methods, and conservation methods for our soil, and forest management, and wildlife conservation and management, our water resources and our mineral resources management. I was looking through the pictures in the book at photographs from 1944 and I saw Bigfoots in the pictures. Someone needs to tell them they have a Bigfoot infestation in the Loblolly pines. I bet there are many pictures of these creatures and folks just do not know about it.

Let's investigate archeological evidence of Bigfoot. Mesopotamia was supposed to be the site of the world's first civilization. Found on Cuneiform Clay Tablets, the Sumerians (Nephilim) were supposedly created by the Annanaki (star people), (sons of God) aka Fallen Angels, who were their gods (with a little g), and the Sumerians were shown to be half God and half man. The Holy Bible confirms this in Chapter 6 of Genesis s as it says "The Sons of God looked down upon the earth and saw that the women of the earth were fair, and came down to them and came unto them and created the Nephilim or Giants, men of great renown who ruled the earth and did evil in the sight of God continually". The Annanaki also made Man and Enkidu. Both were slaves for the Sumerian masters and their gods the Annanaki. Enkidu is Bigfoot. Not in a general term but Bigfoot as in the 10-15-foot large ape like upright creature that is not Sasquatch. Bigfoot can phase out in front of you and disappear from your sight as well as use telepathy to hypnotize or mesmerize you. You may lose time, or forget you saw what you saw. They have special abilities. Bigfoot is an Alien Ape hybrid.

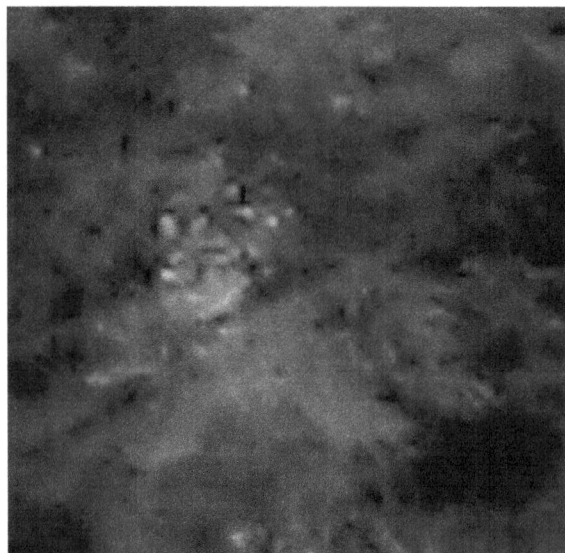

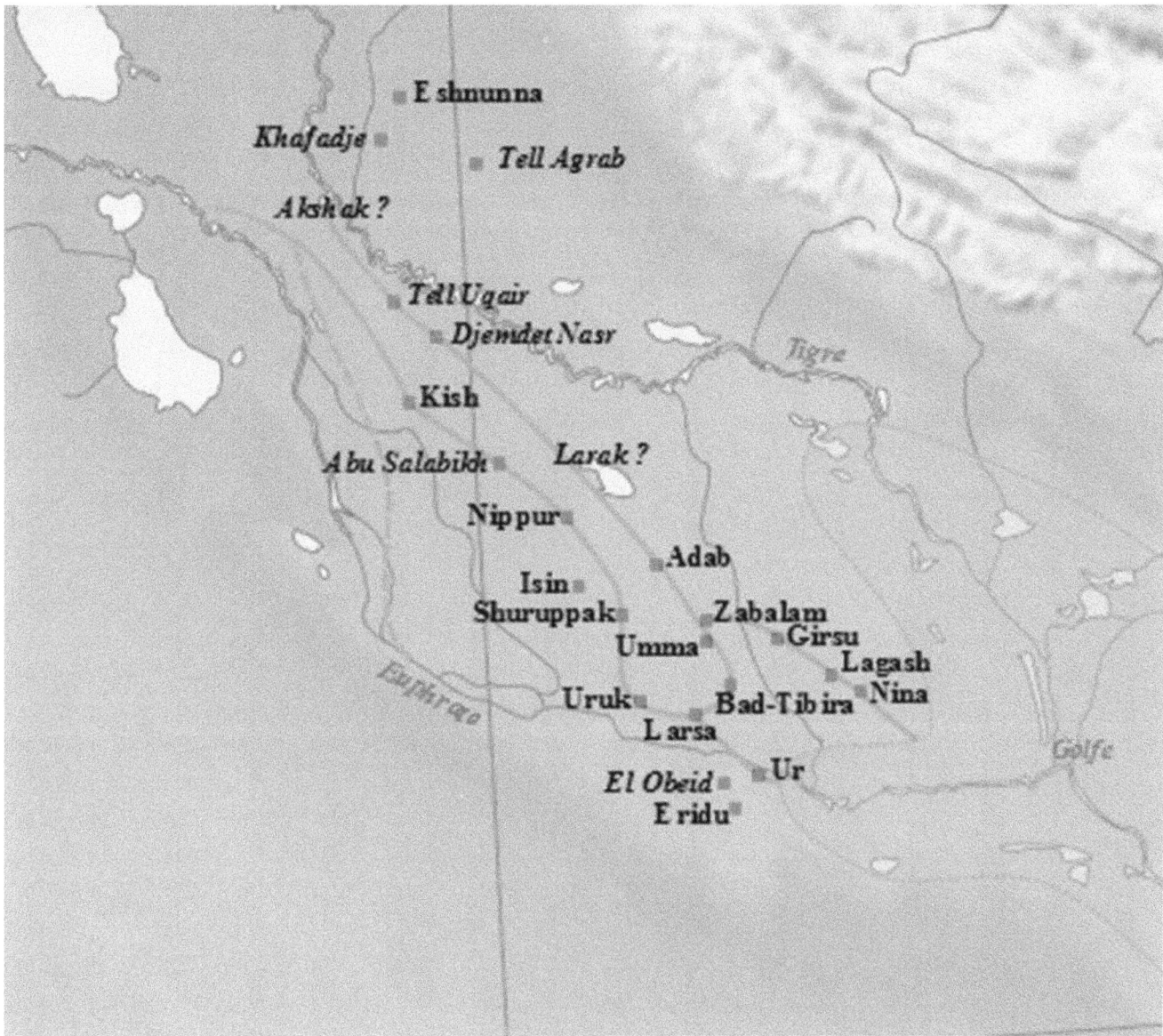

This is the same area the Great Flood with Noah and his ark is placed. The Great Flood came from the breaking of a natural dam that caused the Black Sea to Flood into the Mediterranean Sea and all the counties surrounding it as well as the entire Tigris and Euphrates Valley of Mesopotamia. The secular name for Noah was Gilgamesh and the epic of Gilgamesh describes the Great Flood. It also contains references to Enkidu (Bigfoot) who was friends with Gilgamesh. The secular names for Nephilim are Atlantean (Atlantis), Sumerian, Sons of God, The Watchers (Book of Enoch) and Giants.

The whole known world (The Mediterranean and the Middle East) was almost destroyed. A relic population of Bigfoots and Nephilim must have survived. The book of Enoch which was found in the Dead Sea Scrolls says that the Nephilim were before the flood and some thereafter.

Now to believe all of this you must learn to accept that Genesis is a recreation of what God had destroyed earlier which means it had been created earlier, then destroyed and then recreated again almost exactly 6000 years ago. Sure, the first few sentences of Genesis deals with the overall early creation as well as the book of John (Gospel) in the New Testament which records the actual beginning of time, our time, when the Word of God was with God, and was God (Jesus) and was with God from the beginning. The Word of God created all things for God (Father). Then a few sentences later in Genesis begins the recreation were God receded the waters and then he receded the clouds of a creation that had been destroyed, then recreated by making the earth habitable again. Then in Chapter 6 of Genesis, the Nephilim were doing evil continually , experimenting and creating people with dog heads, and people with bird heads and wings, Bigfoots, and many other oddities found on the walls of Pharos and Kings, People worshiped these creatures also and they became a pantheon of gods and goddesses with all kinds of carnal indulgences which disgusted God and the world was destroyed by the Great Flood about 3000 B.C. when God told Noah to build the Ark. God has destroyed civilization many times and rebuilt it. We know that the earth is 4 billion years old and we know that Adam and Eve (Adamic Man or Homo Sapiens Sapiens) was created just 6000 years ago as the Bible records it.

 Not all of civilization was destroyed nor all Bigfoots and not all Nephilim (Giants) even though the Bible says all life was destroyed. In the original Hebrew Bible, the word for World was Erath which meant the Known World. Have you heard the saying that Alexander the Great conquered the Known World? He did not conquer all of India or go to China. The Scythians and their cavalry of two hundred thousand armored horses and men turned Alexander back form the Steppes of Russia (Scythia). Alexander conquered the whole Middle East and the eastern Mediterranean Sea, Egypt, Libya (Put), Carthage, Phoenicia, Persia, Afghanistan, Eastern Europe, and the Black Sea, all the way to India. The Great Flood was more localized as the King Lists of both China and India was not interrupted and Chinese and Indian records say the flood killed most people who could not get to the mountaintops quick enough.

 Later around 1000 B. C. King David killed Goliath the Giant King of the Philistines. Joab his general killed Goliaths brother and the bible says now all the Giants had been killed off the earth, meaning the Known World. Nephilim continued to live in the new world and ruled many kingdoms.

This is a list of the top ten Giant List that were excavated in the United States over the last 200 years.

1. 18-foot, West Hickory Pennsylvania.
2. 12-foot Lompoc Rancho, California.
3. 10-foot Beaver Lake in the Ozarks, Arkansas.
4. 9-foot 2-inches Catalina Island, California.
5. 8-foot 4-inches San Diego, California.
6. 8-foot 1.5-inches Miamisburg, Ohio. (This skull was more Gorilla Like)
7. 8-foot Steelville, Missouri.
8. 7-foot 6-inches Mounds, Iowa.
9. 7-foot 2-inches Cresap Mound, West Virginia
10. 7-foot Serpent Mound, Ohio

The last king of **Palenque**, seventh century A.D. ruled for 68 years, was a Giant almost 9-foot tall and is most famous for his depiction of a spaceship on the lid to his sarcophagus. Pakal the Great, who reigned from 615 A.D. until his death in 683 A.D., at age of 80. Pakal created a dynasty which he reigned over 6 decades.

Pakal was excavated from his discovered tomb in the 1980's by a Mexican Archeologist. Soon after word was leaked that Pakal was nearly 9-foot-tall, had an elongated nose, head, face, and ears. His nose began in the center of his forehead. He had a strong complexion and had six fingers on each hand, and six toes on each foot. He also had double rows of teeth. The Mexican Government has shut down any information on King Pakal, and there are no photos of him. In 2006 I took a trip to Mexico and went to Tulum, Chechen Itza, and Palenque and took this picture.

The tomb of the Giant was found in a chamber in this Pyramid in the ruins of the city of Palenque, the most fabulous city of the Mayans.

There are about 1000 newspaper reports from the 1800's and the early 1900's showing skeletons of giants along with the people who found them and maybe a local official standing next to the giants. All these accounts and the bodies have mysteriously disappeared after being taken away by the Smithsonian who continue to deny any knowledge of them. Over one thousand pictures in American newspapers all over the United States! Talk about a cover up! And Skeptics always say, where is the body? Where are the bones? How many of these skeletons were Nephilim Giants? How many were Sasquatches, who have very human like bodies and a little more of a Gorilla type head?

Let's make sure of what we have covered so far. First the Annanaki made Man and Bigfoot their slaves. The Bene Ha Elohim (the fallen ones) (Annanaki) or (Watchers) created the Nephilim (sons of the fallen). How can something spiritual mate with something physical? Enoch in the book of the watcher says, "even the angels left their first estate." They left their spiritual bodies for the physical. Jude says they left their heavenly estate. That is how they were able to mate with mankind and create their offspring

Nephilim were treated as gods and became the pantheon of gods worshiped in India, China, Greece, Egypt, and Babylon. At the same time 6000 years ago, God through Jesus Christ (The Word) created Adamic Man (Adam and Eve) in the Eden (valley) of Ararat (Mt. Ararat). We know that this is true biblically as when Cain killed Able (Adams sons). Cain was sentenced to exile and was forced from the garden by two angels with swords of flame to the east to the land of Nod where he married into a wealthy noble, Nephilim family, according to Enoch. This Nephilim society took over the world around the equator building pyramids across the globe.

Remember Nephilim also as Atlantis. Their society was destroyed during the Great Flood. Some Nephilim and their slaves the Bigfoots lived on in the farthest reaches of the world. Bigfoots are not Sasquatches. I use the term Bigfoot to mention all the creatures, but when I individually refer to them, they are separate. Sasquatch is an archaic man. They do not have the ability to disappear or phase out. There are however hybrids.

The Nephilim did create beasts with dog heads, bird heads, and other strange creations. They according to Enoch continued to grow so large they could no longer mate with human women and became homosexuals. It is not hard to go a step further with this thought that they eventually mated with Gigantopithecus Blackie (Bigfoot) to satisfy their lust as they were large enough for them. Also, they wanted their race to continue. It is not inconceivable that they were able to multiply this way as they had previously mated with human women before they grew to large. They have mysterious powers and do not speak. They communicate telepathically and lost their ability to speak. What is the old saying, either use it or lose it? They can phase almost completely out making themselves invisible. For these revelations the book of Enoch was omitted from our Bibles even though Jesus referenced the Book of Enoch as well as Jude.

American Indians had legends about these creatures before there was any one name given for such creatures. The details differed in their descriptions from region to region. Most cultures around the world have myths of giant human like creatures in their folk history. Each native American language has its own name for the creatures. Hairy Man, Wild Man, and Wood knocker are just a few of the names given. Some accounts describe cannibalistic wild men that live on top of Mt. St. Helens and the surrounding area. Less scary descriptions come from upper Washington State tell of hairy men that were nocturnal and would steal salmon out of their fishing nets at night.

Bigfoot cave art from the American West, estimated by some to be at least 2000 years old. Picture taken by me on a trip out west to the Tule River Indian Reservation in Portersville, California.

This picture, below, was taken on my trip out west. On my way back, I went through Mt. Zion National Park.

Very large grey and reddish-brown Bigfoots in the back of the picture. Mothers and babies sitting in the foreground.

About 33% of all reported sightings have come from the northwest. The rest of the sightings are scattered across the rest of the United States. Other Hot Spots for sightings include rural Pennsylvania, and the Great Lakes region in rural areas, and parts of the Southeastern United States. The descriptions vary amongst the tribes; however, commonalities include the ability to disappear right in front of you, and the ability to mesmerize you into not seeing them, or to hypnotize you into forgetting what you saw. Also, that they can shapeshift and look like other animals. These things are true as I have witnessed it myself. I am in contact with Bigfoots and Skunk Apes daily and Sasquatches every couple of months. This is one reason why I believe in the Ancient Alien theory that also has biblical backup, that the Annanaki created Bigfoot using gene splicing. They may have taken Gigantopithecus, the largest Ape every recorded, and added DNA to make him walk upright and more intelligent. Later the Sons of the Fallen mated with the Bigfoot to create huge Giants that they are today which gave them strange unnatural powers.

Jane Goodall, primatologist, told National Public Radio "Well now, you will be amazed when I tell you that I'm sure that they exist (referring to Bigfoot). Dmitri Bayanov, Chairman of Hominology, The Darwin Museum in Moscow says "All researchers versed in this science do know that Bigfoot is a mammal, not a myth, because of the females' conspicuous mammae (breasts). All know that Bigfoot is a primate because of the dermal ridges on the sole of its feet."

Bigfoots at Mt. Zion National Park

Here is a very recent photo I took of a very large Primate that is nearly 17-foot tall and has a protruding mouth. This is Gigantopithecus Blackie x Alien DNA x Nephilim= Hybrid (aka. Bigfoot), I do believe! How Majestic, How Impressive. I spoke to them on top of Hall Hill, and told them Hi, and that I like them, and that I would come back soon to visit. All of this while sitting in my car. Some in the back of the picture are over 25-foot tall! Are they the Giant Nephilim? Do all the others serve them? Now you see why the Sasquatches are armed! The Sasquatches work together as an army and well-armed and with tactics as well.

Gigantopithecus Blackie

This is an example of Bigfoots phasing out. Almost all the ones in my yard are Bigfoots.

Gigantopithecus Blackie

After running this through a sauna filter, they show much better. Let's look at another example.

Here is an unfiltered image that looks like a bunch of brush. After filtering it with a mercury filter, they come into better view.

The green arrows point to Giants, at least 22 to 25 feet tall. Are they Nephilim? The yellow arrows point to Bigfoots. There are no sasquatches here. I believe that the Giants are worshiped as Gods while the others do all the work.

Unknown Bipeds are represented here by the Giants in the background and this creature in the water that looks as if he has horns. This is truly a bunch of misfits and outcasts, a motley crew for sure.

Here is a Nephilim Giant with his Bigfoot wife and children. By now I'm sure that all the Bigfoot race has Nephilim in them which is part human as the Nephilim were created by fallen angels and human women.

Well, I have said it! I have been beating around the bush long enough and now I must deal with this. I have been avoiding the subject for long enough and have almost completed two books but can go no longer without saying it. The reason that governments deny Bigfoot is the same reason they have special powers. They are Ancient Alien Hybrids according to the Ancient Alien Theory. I just replace that term with Angels and Demons, and it explains everything. There is more proof of this from the ancient city of Tiwanaku, in the highlands of western Bolivia near Lake Titicaca and Puma Punku. Structures excavated include the Acapana which is a sunken court. A staircase with sculptures placed in the eastern wall show all the races of men as well as alien races of humanoids. There is a head sculpture of an Alien Grey, and a Reptilian and others. We are not alone. Archeology, History, and the Bible as well as Enoch tell of the invasion of the Star People who came to earth and mated with the people of the earth and created other races either through DNA manipulation and or physical mating. What else can explain beings that are physical, but they can disappear before your eyes. What else could explain the tremendous size of these Giants in the background with a normal sized Bigfoot standing near the center of this picture which I took in my friends back yard. He and his wife live 13 miles from me but when I pulled up, I noticed they were keying on me. I guess they have heard of me also.

These guys were on the corner of my house near the eve of the roof in my crepe myrtle. They must want their candy peanut bars.

Sasquatches

Sasquatches are human. I believe that they are Homo Rhodesiensis, also known as Denisovan man. Denisovan Man is one of a variety of archaic humans living contemporary to and predating the emergence of the earliest anatomically modern humans, Homo Sapiens. Their mouths protrude but very little. Their bodies look very manlike except they grow up to ten foot tall. Now we get to talk about Archaic Humans and trace the hominid Sasquatch back through time to understand his origins.

As you can see, the Sasquatches are more human looking that the Bigfoot. It is because they are human. The term Archaic Humans generally refer to Homo Neanderthalensis, Homo Rhodesiensis (Denisovans), and Homo Heidelbergensis, and Homo Antecessor. Archaic humans had a brain size averaging 1200 to 1400 cubic centimeters which is in the range of modern-day humans. The differences are thicker, more robust skulls, and thicker brow ridges. What is interesting to note is that modern human's brow ridges grow with age. If modern man were to live if he did in the days of old, his brow ridges would match that of archaic humans. Man's life span was shortened to 120 years according to the bible just a few generations after the Great Flood. Non-Modern varieties of Homo continued to exist up and until 10,000 years ago. According to recent genetic studies, modern humans have bred with at least two types of archaic humans; Denisovans and Neanderthals.

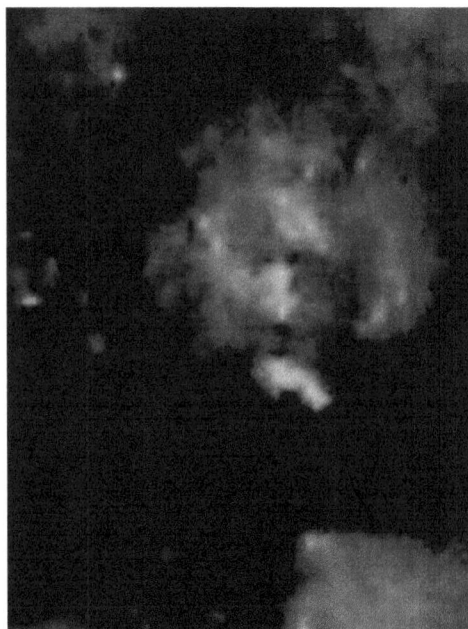

As recently as 11,500 years ago the Red Deer Cave People of Central China, according to Chris Stringer of the Natural History Museum of London suggested that Denisovans mated with modern humans. The evolutionary lines between archaic humans and modern humans and archaic humans and the earlier Homo Erectus is not defined. We know for a fact after mapping the genome of modern humans that northern Europeans contain on average 1-4% of their DNA is Neanderthal suggesting that one of the reasons of Neanderthals extinction is due to being absorbed into modern man's DNA by inbreeding. In the east the Melanesian islanders of the Solomon Islands have up to 6% Denisovan DNA. The people of New Guinea and the Australian Aborigines have between 4-6% Denisovan in their DNA. The Denisovans are considered cousins of the Neanderthals with both groups migrating out of Africa to Central Asia with Neanderthals heading west to Europe and Denisovans heading to the East from there about 400,000 to 100,000 years ago. This is based on scientific evidence of a fossil found in southern Siberia. The evidence from Melanesia suggests their origin came from central and southeast Asia before migrating by sea to the Solomon Islands.

The Tibetan people as well as their neighbors, the Sherpa of Nepal have a significant amount of Denisovan in their DNA. The Tibetan people diverged from the Sherpa people about 11,500 years ago and have genetic affinities to three different archaic human populations: Denisovans,

Neanderthals, and yet an unidentified archaic human group. The Tibetan people have about 6% Denisovan DNA. The Sherpas of Nepal have 6-8% Denisovan DNA. There are many more studies to be done especially in the Siberian Region.

Denisovans and Neanderthals split from Homo Sapiens about 600,000 years ago and they split from each other about 200,000 years ago. Modern humans, Neanderthal and Denisovan shared a common ancestor about 1,000,000 years ago. There are legends of wild people in the Caucus mountain region, Pakistan, the Altai mountains, Mongolia, Central Asia, The Himalayas, the Ural Mountains in Russia, and the Carpathian Mountains. These creatures in Asia are known as Almas, or Alma, Almac, Almaste, and Albus.

In a traditional Tibetan medical book, the Materia Medica, used by Tibetans and Mongolians included drawings of Almases and thousands of other faunae are in the book and not one mythological animal is included in the book. British Anthropologist, Myra Shackley noted "all of the creatures are living and observable today."

The story of Zana and Khwit

In 1850 in the autonomous Abkhazia region of northwestern Georgia in the Caucus Mountain region, a female Almas (wild woman) was captured in the mountains. She at first was angry and violent with her captors but after three years she settled down to her captivity, Zana soon became domesticated and assisted with simple household chores. She had sexual relations with men of the village and her first four children died from exposure as she still lived outside, slept in a hole that she dug that had a roof over it. The women of the village began taking her children from her and four survived and were raised as humans. They were functional in society, marrying and having children of their own. Although there were slight differences in their appearance and mental capabilities, they were able to function as normal humans. Zana died in 1890. Many attempts by Russian Zoologists to find and exhume her grave failed. Khwit her younger son graduated from high school, held a job, married and raised a family. He was very tall and strong, like his mother, but his facial features looked more like his father. Khwit died in 1954. His grave was marked and easily found, and his skull was exhumed and sent to Moscow for study. The skull was studied by two Anthropologists M.A. Kolodieva and M.M. Gerasimova. The report was given to the Relic Hominid Research Seminar and the Moscow Naturalists Society and published in 1987 by Igor Bourtsev who worked many years on many trips to Abkhazia to look for Zana's grave. It was then Bourtsev decided to exhume the skull of Khwit whose grave was well marked as his family he sired continued to visit his grave. Professor N. Bourchak-Abramovich assisted Bourtsev in the digging of Khwit's grave. The skull of Khwit caused great excitement among anthropologists as it exhibited a combination of ancient and modern features.

Anthropologist M.A. Kolodieva indicated that Khwit's skull was significantly different from other skulls from the Abkhazia region. She said his skull most closely resembles the Neolithic Vounigi II skulls of the fossil series...

Brian Sykes of the University of Oxford in 2013 tested Khwit's molar tooth and determined through his mitochondrial DNA that Khwit was 50 percent Russian and 50 percent Sub-Saharan African and that his mother Zana was 100 percent African, but of no known group. The Ottoman Turks had an empire that included all of Northern Africa in the 1800's and had brought slaves to the Abkhazia region. A few of the slaves did escape but not enough to produce a viable breeding population. This did not set well with Sykes especially after examining the skull which he said had both modern and ancient characteristics. In 2015 Brian Sykes went back to Abkhazia and tested living relatives of Khwit and determined that the Sub-Saharan African DNA was of 100,000-year-old relic stock that left Africa eons ago and lived in the Caucus Mountain Region for many generations.

Mo Cho Rook aka Brutus with a spear and club with twine around his neck tied to the neck of his club. This photo filtered in septia tone.

This Photo is filtered with a mercury filter. To me this Sasquatch is an Archaic Human that makes tools and weapons as deadly as the American Indian's weapons. His hands have the dexterity to make precise tools and weapons. The spear is straight and smooth. The spear tip is tall and sharp. His club has a large stiff handle and the club has a bulbus end. The club is smooth as if sanded down like a woodworker would. Bigfoots do not have this ability to make such tools as they do not have hands that can work the wood with such dexterity. Bigfoots are not human. Sasquatches are human. Bigfoots do not vocalize like the Sasquatches do. They do not have a voice box larynx like humans do. Sasquatches have an entire language and form sentences, Bigfoots are telepathic and can only grunt and squeal. Bigfoots lack the ability of fine precision tool making as their hands are not human. The Sasquatches make precision tools and are quite capable of using them. Bigfoots can become 20 plus feet tall. Sasquatches are 8 to

9-foot-tall with some attaining 10- foot- tall. Bigfoots jawline is extended outward and down. Sasquatches barely have what could be considered a muzzle, Bigfoots can make themselves disappear in plain view, Sasquatches must hide in brush to not be seen. Bigfoots can phase out even on camera. Sasquatches if caught in the open can be filmed and photographed.

There is a book that my friend with the BFRO, Carter Brushardt, told me about titled *My 50 Years with Bigfoot*, that was published by Mary Green Publishing; written by Mary A. Green and Co-Authored by Janice Carter Coy. Published in Cookeville, Tennessee, the book is about Mr. Robert Carter Sr., and his granddaughters Janice and Lilla Carter's experiences living on the family farm and co-habituating with Bigfoots on their land. I would like to thank them for documenting and writing about their experiences and providing Mr. Robert's glossary of terms (words) which helped me learn to communicate with Brutus and Scar in the Sasquatch language. The pictures of their farm showed a lot of Bigfoots and the highlighted film on their YouTube video of Fox, in my opinion, is that Fox was a Sasquatch. Fox was Mr. Robert Carter's friend who he communicated with. Bigfoots and Sasquatches all live together and hunt together and the Sasquatches organize the hunts. Sasquatches are the organizers and communicators of the bunch.

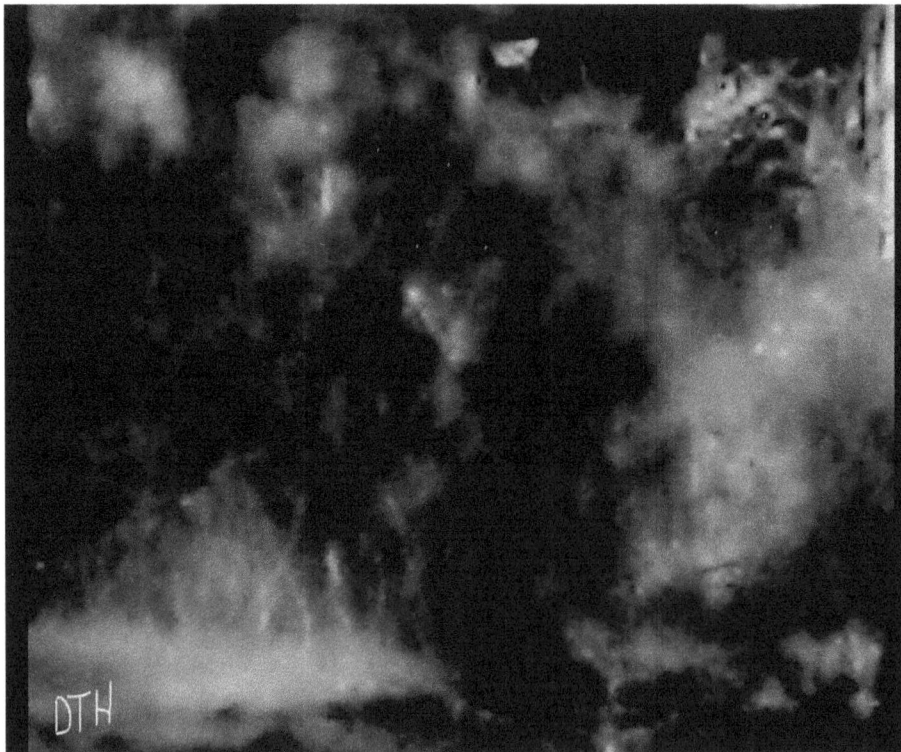

Bigfoots on Hall Hill, Kisatchie National Forest. Scar the Sasquatch Hybrid is their leader.

In 1420 Hans Schiltberger recorded his personal observation of Almases that had been captured by the Mongols. He was on an expedition to Mongolia and was taken prisoner by the Mongol Khan. He kept a journal of his trip and recorded seeing a man and a woman covered in hair and that they were savages that lived up in the mountains. Schiltberger also is credited with sighting the famous Przewalski horses as the first European to do so. The Mongol Khan gave the Almases as a gift to a local viceroy. The Manuscript of his documented travels are in the Munich Municipal Library.

Example of Bigfoots phasing out till they are almost invisible.

As you can see there is historical and archeological evidence of Bigfoot and Sasquatch. I haven't even come close to telling it all as there is so much information about the subject and that is not the purpose of this book. The purpose of this book is to show my evidence and to discuss my observations on the subject. These Guys are my friends. They crave my attention and follow me around as I work in my yard. Some stay an extended time here and then are replaced by others who have heard about me.

Also, I hope you can see that Bigfoots are different than Sasquatches and I hope I have shown those differences. The other thing I would like to show to the reader is that Bigfoots have special powers and can disappear in plain sight. They are allowing me to see them and I think that is a blessing.

Sources:

Wikipedia

In the footsteps of the Russian Snowman by Demetri Bayanov, 1996 Moscow Russia.

British Anthropologist Myra Shackley, *Still Living?*

My 50 years with Bigfoot, Mary A. Green and Janice Carter Coy.

The Holy Bible

The Book of Enoch

Discovery Channel 4 documentary *Bigfoot Files.* Brian Sykes

Chariots of the Gods, Erick Von Daniken, the creator of Ancient Alien Theory

Observations and Interpretations and photos provided by me, David T. Hollis

Hey, at least I have an explanation. Most just deny because it is easier!

David Hollis grew up and graduated High School in Louisiana, where he was an avid hunter and fisherman in his youth. He graduated with a B.A. from The University of Mississippi; double majoring in History and Political Science that served as a Pre-Law Degree. David started out in the professional world in Retail Store Management, District Manager, Manager of Sales Operations, and lastly General Manager of Sales for BellSouth Cellular Corporation. His management skills are:

1. Observational Skills so feedback can be given on performance issues

2. Documentation skills so that feedback cannot be denied

3. Planning and Goal Setting Skills

4. Research and Implementation Skills

5. Ability to motivate employees to a high degree of productivity. Initiates the activity level without supervision.

All these skills entered his project.

My friends at Dartigo swamp coming out on the road to greet me.

Dartigo Swamp. Can you see my friends?

These are Bigfoots.

I entered the woods to sit with my friends. These are Sasquatches in the foreground.

Look in the top of the tree on the left. There looks to be a young albino female Sasquatch atop the tree. This is virgin forest that supports the most abundant life. All the species are represented here.

They all say goodbye.

The Bigfoots in my yard say bye!

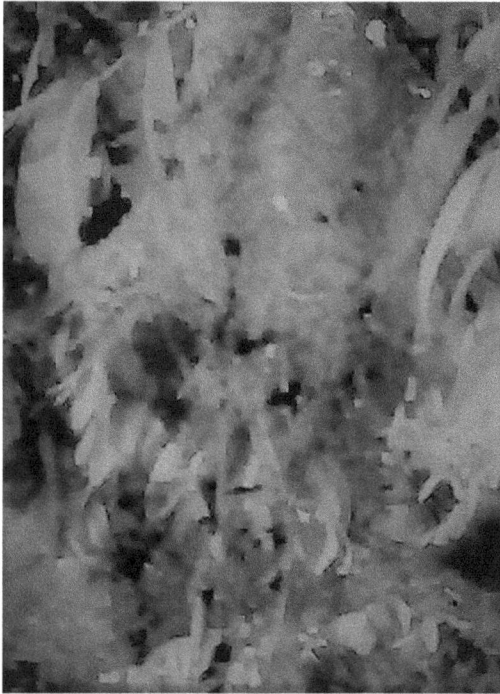

Goodbye from the unknown bipeds.

Just making sure!

A group of Skunk Apes. A juvenile has a Blue Winged Teal as a pet riding on his head. How peaceful they must be.

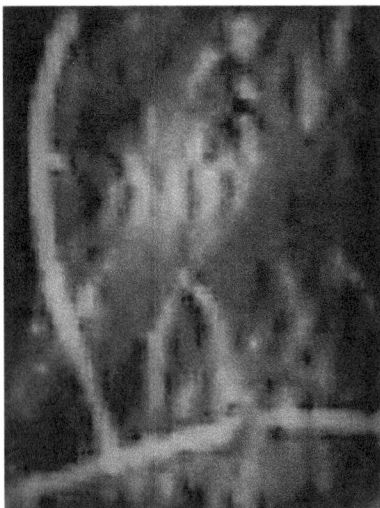

A close-up of the Blue Winged Teal. He says Goodbye! I know it is a lot to take in. I believe that if you are pleasing to GOD that he gives you your heart's desire. What else could explain all of this? This journey is not over and there is no telling where it will take me. Thank you, my Lord and Master, that you are keeping my life vibrant and my mind open to all the possibilities in this world, and in the vast universe you created, and in the future when you will elevate man even over the angels and put us in charge of your perfect creation. Help us Lord to attain that, Glory. Amen